Do-It-Yourself Retirement

Retiring Sooner

How to Accelerate
Your Financial Independence

Darrow Kirkpatrick

StructureByDesign

Chattanooga, Tennessee 37405

ISBN: 978-0-9892830-0-7

www.CanIRetireYet.com

Dedication

To Caroline and Alex

Disclaimer

The content here contains personal opinions of the author regarding financial and economic matters. It is for educational purposes only. The publisher and author do not imply or intend any guarantee of accuracy. The information here is not necessarily suitable for every individual: Use it at your own risk. No guarantees are made that you will achieve results similar to those described here, or any specific results whatsoever from using the concepts and approaches discussed. No guarantees are implied or expressed. Though reasonable effort has been taken to make this material as useful as possible, there may be typographical mistakes or errors in the content. Neither the author nor the publisher is engaged in rendering professional services including, but not limited to, accounting, tax, legal, or investment planning. This information is not intended as a substitute for such professional services. If specific advice is needed or appropriate, the reader should seek out and engage a licensed professional. The author and publisher specifically disclaim any liability, loss or risk taken by readers who directly or indirectly act on this information. You are solely responsible for your own decisions and actions, and their results.

Contents

Introduction

"People pursuing financial independence are first and foremost pursuing independence. The financial independence is just a subset. Anyone thinking that early retirement is the primary objective is not getting it. Retirement is not the point. Freedom is."
— Jacob Lund Fisker

For most of human history nobody considered the possibility of early retirement. Financial independence was reserved for royalty, while the rest of humanity worked until they were too old or sick to support themselves, hoping family would care for them at that point. Even now, the vast majority of workers don't envision the possibility of early retirement. Most work until their 60's or later, stuck in a lifestyle they inherited instead of chose, unconscious of other options.

However, new financial services and technological productivity in the modern world make early retirement accessible. Anybody willing to put in the effort to master the techniques of financial independence, and apply them over a sufficient period of time, can achieve financial freedom.

Whether you love your current job or not, wouldn't it be

nice to do your work when and where you please, a little or a lot, to suit your own schedule and interests? Maybe you'd rather work part time, or do something different that pays less or not at all? Well, you can do that, and more, by achieving financial independence and retiring sooner.

This book lays the groundwork for your financial freedom, then helps you get there quicker. In the chapters that follow I will teach you to assess where you are on the path to financial independence and early retirement, to define your own retirement goals, and to choose and use the best tools to reach that vision. I will also offer dozens of practical tips and techniques, based on my own experience, for accelerating that process. The fact is, you can speed up your retirement by years, or even decades, in some cases.

This book is for the person who intends to pilot his or her own ship to retirement. Doing retirement planning and money management *yourself* is simply the quickest way to financial independence because it will cost less, and the journey will be tuned to your own needs and capabilities. Your savings represent your accumulated life energy, and your future freedom. There is no one who can exercise the same care with your wealth that *you* can. I strongly encourage you not to relinquish the key decision-making around your money.

Finally, remember that retirement, even early financial independence, is still a *long-term* process. Some short-cuts are available, but there is no magic. Enjoy every day of the journey. It's not worth it to retire earlier, only to realize that you've sacrificed years of happiness to get there.

Overview

The book is divided into four main sections. In the first section I explore your "financial dashboard" – your expenses, savings, and net worth – the most important progress indicator. This section helps you accurately snapshot your current economic state, and monitor its progress.

In the next section I explore the concept of "retirement" and how it applies to you. It's essential to understand your goal in detail if you want to plan how to arrive there in advance. In this section we explore retirement lifestyles, how much money may be required, and where it will come from.

Next, I explore the tools needed to achieve your retirement goals. We review the different vehicles for saving your money, and the financial services you'll need for help along the way. I also briefly discuss passive index investing, the best investing approach for most individual investors, and the related concepts of asset allocation and rebalancing.

Note: This is not an investing book. Perhaps it comes as a surprise, but great investing prowess is not necessary to retire early. The most important thing is to avoid major mistakes. And passive index investing is the best way for most of us to reach our goals safely.

Finally, I conclude with invaluable tips and techniques for *accelerating* your retirement, right now. I explore the mathematical relationship between savings rates and years needed to retire, and show the dramatic shortcuts available by improving your savings rate. Then I present a series of powerful tips for decreasing your expenses, and accelerating your savings, to build wealth and retire sooner.

My Story

I grew up in a Navy family where I learned integrity, economy, and the value of work. I'm an Eagle Scout, and I graduated with a degree in Civil Engineering. Soon after college I discovered personal computers, and got in on the ground floor of that revolution.

I started my own software company, which I eventually sold to a pioneer in numerical modeling for PC's. That company, Haestad Methods, eventually sold to Bentley Systems – a global leader in architecture and engineering software. I retired from Bentley in the Spring of 2011 after 29 years of programming, designing, and managing computer software development.

I began serious saving and investing in my mid-30's. I was 50 when I retired, financially independent, with a net worth well over $1 million. We own our house free and clear, and have no debt of any kind.

I'm not a dot-com millionaire. And I didn't become financially independent by flipping real estate or trading hot stocks. I did it the traditional way: hard work, frugality, prudent investing, and patience.

I'm an engineer, not a salesperson or a financial advisor. When it comes to money, my top priorities are simplicity, reliability, and safety. Now my mission is to help others become financially independent as I did, through writing about personal finance.

The book you are about to read is as much financial autobiography as it is a personal finance book. It's the story of how I did, and do, things. It's a story worth reading, because I succeeded in retiring at age 50 with a lifestyle of my choosing. But it's still just *one* story. Yours will be different. I had some good fortune that others won't get. Others will receive breaks that I didn't get. And we'll all experience a collection of life's curve balls that none of us expected or planned for....

The perspective here is individual, independent, and idiosyncratic. Much of what I do, and did, is mainstream personal finance philosophy, but some things are not. I live very frugally in most areas and lavishly in a few. I also willingly take on certain expenses and risks to keep my life simple. For example, I eschew some forms of insurance, and don't believe in sinking lots of money into a home. I'm negative on complicated tax deductions and IRA conversions. I find that the complexity added to your life often obscures the benefits, if any, that are provided.

So don't expect to do everything the way I did. And, if you do, don't expect to get the same results. We each walk our own path, subject to our own environment and our own history. Some will succeed in retiring earlier. Some will have to work longer. But I am confident that if you'll choose from among the good ideas here, the ones that make sense to you, and apply them to suit your own life, you'll come out far ahead of where you might have been.

I believe the lessons I've learned in achieving financial independence will help speed your own passage. The path to financial independence begins with education and awareness, and ends with the freedom to live and work however you choose. Best wishes on your journey!

PART ONE: YOUR FINANCIAL DASHBOARD

"The connection between pre-retirement and retirement isn't built with more (or less) savings. It is built by becoming a student of how you spend your money today. Only when you know that will you have the reassurance that you're on track."
— Scott Burns

In this first section of the book we'll explore how you can become more aware of your expenses, your savings, and the growing net worth that will provide your retirement nest egg. Here we'll identify, explain, and discuss the key indicators or metrics you should monitor – why they matter, and how to calculate them. When we're done, you'll know everything you need to compute these simple values on your own, or choose software to do it for you.

These are the same indicators I used and refined from the time I began serious saving and investing around age 35, until I retired financially independent at age 50. These measures helped me stay on course, stay off the shoals of financial disaster, and optimize my own journey to financial independence. They can do the same for you!

An airplane can't be flown without an array of instruments. Driving an automobile without a working speedometer, fuel gauge, or odometer would be ill-advised. Even a walk in the woods is safer and more enjoyable with at least a map, a watch, and perhaps a compass.

Similarly, your journey to financial independence will be smoother and more efficient if you can tell where you're headed, and how fast. How much do you spend? How much have you saved? Is that value going up or down? Just as you wouldn't drive a car without a dashboard, you need a "financial dashboard" that provides you the key information for financial decision-making, allowing you to navigate your financial life from early to mid career, to retirement, and beyond.

1. Know Your Expenses

First, I'm going to let you in on a little debate in the personal finance world: A prominent blogger and author writes that most people won't even *bother* to read books that tell them they need to track what they spend, because it makes them feel guilty. On the other side, a prominent financial advisor and leader in retirement research writes that there isn't even any point in trying to *do* retirement planning if somebody can't figure out his or her basic expenses!

You probably sense which side of this debate I'm on. More important than my opinion is this simple fact: You can't possibly retire early and safely, without a deep understanding of your expenses. There is simply too much risk that you'll run out of money otherwise. And you'll get to retirement much faster in the first place, if you have complete knowledge and control of your expenses. So guess what? In my book, tracking expenses comes first. I'm betting, and hoping, you'll come along for the ride. The end result will be worth it!

Becoming Aware

Retirement or financial independence begins with awareness of your true needs and wants. To be financially independent means to be able to pay for all your living expenses from your *savings* – investments and retirement benefits. There are essentially three variables in this equation: your expenses, your savings, and the rate of return you are able to achieve on your savings. Of those variables, expenses are most easily under your control. (Savings is also under your control – but is difficult and time-consuming to increase. Investment returns are only partially under your control. Much of the time, they will be subject to forces beyond you.)

So, like it or not, you simply can't retire if you don't know how much it costs you to live. That applies whether you are a 60-year-old kindergarten teacher, a 45-year-old mechanical engineer, or a 30-year-old Internet tycoon. Your cost of living dictates your required income, and your required income dictates your required savings. Only by having that knowledge of your required savings can you say whether financial independence is imminent, possible, or a long ways off.

Your cost of living is one of the most personal and variable parameters in the retirement equation. We all know, when we stop to think about it, that money doesn't buy happiness. And we all probably know a spectrum of individuals, or couples, who live under a range of economic circumstances, with varying and uncorrelated degrees of happiness.

I think it's possible for different couples in the U.S. to live on anywhere from about $2,000/month to about $10,000/month, without a great deal of measurable difference in happiness or satisfaction. And, while most of us will fall somewhere in the middle of that range, it is well within our power to optimize our needs and ratchet down our wants in order to live on less, and thus reach financial independence sooner.

But in order to control your expenses this way, you must first be aware of and understand them. You can't control or optimize what you can't measure – and so financial independence begins with measuring your cost of living.

Many spending decisions are emotional – they can reflect our deepest desires and fears. Tracking your money helps to create awareness, which leads you to the essential reasons you spend, and control over your emotions. Once you become aware of your spending, you can begin to make intelligent choices about whether it fits in with your personal ideals, financial priorities, and long term goals – or whether you are letting emotions override your own best interests. Over the long haul, being aware of your spending is one of the most important actions you can take to build wealth and retire comfortably!

To further convince yourself of the benefits of tracking expenses, ask yourself whether any small business can function without that information. A business that doesn't know its expenses is at severe risk of cash flow problems or, worst case, bankruptcy. If it spends more than it takes in over any substantial period of time, it will run out of the cash needed to stock inventory, pay utilities, and meet payroll. The solution is to track expenses and understand costs precisely. Shouldn't you run your personal life the same way? Granted, you don't have shareholders or investors watching over your shoulder, expecting a profit. But you *do* have obligations to yourself and your family. Why not take the best approaches from running a small business and apply them to your personal finances so you can enjoy more of the good things in life?

If that's not enough, here are three other good reasons to keep track of your expenses, each of which will allow you to retire sooner:

1. By committing a small amount of time now, you will save huge amounts of wasted time later worrying about your finances and trying to make ends meet.

2. It's highly likely you'll discover hidden costs ripe for savings – small amounts that add up over time, or major purchases that can be economized or deferred.

3. Understanding your expenses today will help you control and reduce your expenses once you retire.

So we've discussed the rationale for, and value in, tracking or measuring expenses. But how do you begin? For some individuals, tracking their every expense might come naturally. But for most of us, even an engineer like me, it's a habit that must be learned. And even for those of us who are willing and able to track most of our expenses, some sort of system is required to manage all the data efficiently, without it becoming a burden. So next we'll discuss two possible approaches, depending on your level of commitment, and the accuracy desired: *Real Time Tracking or One-Time Analysis.*

Real-Time Tracking

Let's begin by discussing the most accurate approach to monitoring expenses, and the best investment of your time for the long haul: real-time tracking. This means you are putting in place a system to track all your expenses, as they occur, or shortly thereafter, on some periodic basis. This is the "best" approach by most standards because the information is most accurate and will always be up to date. You will always have the best information for making personal finance decisions.

But first, let's deal with some objections:

Objection #1: I don't have time for this.

I use a very refined and detailed tracking system. In seconds I can tell you how much we spent on groceries, or gas, for the month to date or any month in the last two decades. I can look at our accounts and know how much cash we have on hand and when we might need to replenish it under different scenarios. This system takes me about two hours each week to maintain. You could cut some corners, if desired, and take less time. I have saved many thousands of dollars over the years by carefully watching where our money goes; and I retired early. The payback has been clear. If the goal is important to you, you'll find an hour or two a week to achieve it.

Objection #2: I don't want penny-pinching to take all the fun out of living.

Tracking expenses is about the big picture. It's possible that you are spending so much on small splurges that you can't meet your financial goals, but I wouldn't start by looking there. If at all possible, you *need* small treats, and you *don't* need to micromanage *small* sums of money, to meet your major financial goals.

The best thing I ever did to encourage tracking our expenses was to set an informal "bother threshold." If you're a college student or a compulsive spender it might need to be fairly low. If you're relatively wealthy or inherently frugal it can be higher. For me, in the early days it was a few dollars.

Now it's about $5 to $10.

Here's how it works: When something costs less than that threshold, I pay cash and don't bother getting a receipt or keeping track.

I've always told myself that if it ever appeared there were large sums of money unaccounted for in our spending, I could revisit this threshold, and lower it – but that's never happened. I have a "Miscellaneous" category in our budget where I record the total cash withdrawn and spent each month. That Miscellaneous category remains at about *one percent* of our monthly spending. Meanwhile, by not tracking small cash purchases, I've cut out dozens of trivial transactions each year that I didn't need to monitor, or feel guilty about – and left room for more joy in life.

(Note: The strict definition of the word "budget" above implies *estimated* or *future* expenses, but I will also frequently use the term to simply describe our average *current* expenses. A "budget," to me, is simply what it costs you to live, by category.)

Objection #3: I don't want to be one of those money geeks who collects receipts or jots down every purchase in a little notebook.

Thanks to modern technology, you very rarely need to track your expenses manually at the time they occur. The vast majority of your expenses can go on debit or credit cards (paid off every month!) and can be routed to your personal computer where they can be categorized quickly and sometimes automatically. Being the careful type, I generally do collect receipts and enter them in the computer over the course of the month, before statements arrive. I like to monitor our cash flow, and have this additional check against potential fraud or bank errors. But that step is entirely optional. Many people now simply download their transactions to their computer, or review them over the Internet, and check and categorize them that way. This is perfectly adequate.

The same principles apply to check writing. In today's world, you can minimize your need to even write checks. The vast majority of your expenses can be paid by debit/credit cards or electronic funds transfer. For those remaining few checks you must write each month – small donations or personal services – you can make the same choice as for credit card receipts. If you want to track your money carefully, jot down the check in your check register and enter it into the computer when you get the chance. Or simply wait until the end of the month and download the transaction along with your statement.

Desktop Software

I'm assuming that everyone will use a computer to track expenses. To solve a modern problem – retiring early – use the best modern tools. Achieving financial independence requires every instrument at your disposal.

Many will choose to track their finances on the web, and I'll discuss that in a moment. But popular options for desktop-based personal finance software – meaning your data stays on your computer, not the Internet – include *You Need a Budget*, *Moneydance,* and *Quicken*.

Quicken is the personal finance software that I can recommend from personal experience. For me, and many others, Quicken may be the oldest PC application in continuous use. I switched to Quicken from my own checkbook register program in 1989 and never looked back. It has competently tracked our spending and savings, balanced our accounts, and kept an eye on our budget for more than two decades now. Quicken is one of the software applications that I would truly dread living without.

For what it's worth, I forgo Quicken's extensive online banking features. I'm not keen on having the software automatically stuff transactions into my carefully kept accounts. Though, as written above, I think online banking is a good option for most users.

It is hard to imagine living in the modern world without a money management program, and Quicken is one of the best. Unfortunately the program appeared to peak in the mid-1990s, and has been coasting for a while. The Quicken of today is not always the fast, seamless, trustworthy application of yesterday. And Intuit seems to have been distracted by its many other businesses in recent years. So, while I can still recommend Quicken, you owe it to yourself to review other options as well.

Web Software

Many mainstream software applications have moved to

the web in the last decade, and personal finance is no exception. Internet security has made great strides. Financial services are at the forefront of security and now use multiple sophisticated mechanisms to keep information private. If you take reasonable precautions with your passwords, the chances of an account being compromised are very small. Yet a small percent of us will probably never feel comfortable consolidating *all* of our personal finance information online. The consequences of having our entire financial life compromised are not worth the benefits. But for many others, especially those just starting out, and those with simple finances, the web is the easiest route to tracking your financial life.

One of the leading sites is Mint.com (also owned by Intuit) and, since it's free (with advertising or product "recommendations"), there is no reason not to check it out. Mint brings all your financial accounts together in one place to automatically categorize transactions, help you set budgets, and let you achieve savings goals. It begins with the ability to connect to most every U.S. financial institution so you can download your data automatically. This gives Mint the ability to display all your information in one place: checking, savings, credit cards, loans, investments, etc. Those concerned about security will rest easier knowing that Mint is "read-only" – nobody can withdraw or move funds using the site.

Mint has powerful capabilities for automatically categorizing transactions – though you should expect to fine-tune these by hand, especially when you split one transaction across several categories – as might be the case when you buy groceries and other supplies at the same store. Mint automatically averages spending in different categories to help you create a budget, and lets you create one-time savings goals.

Mint specializes in providing *alerts.* For example, it will warn you if you're headed over budget, remind you of bills due, or inform you of fees. And, if desired, the Mint mobile apps for iPhone and Android will let you enter transactions right after you make purchases.

Should you try Mint, here are a couple of caveats: don't let its budget alerts turn you off the program. Simply turn *them off* if they are disillusioning or annoying. Tracking your spending is too valuable a function to be spoiled by nagging software. In the same vein, go slowly in using Mint to track your investments. As we'll discuss later in the book, you don't need constant updates on your portfolio value to be a successful investor. In fact, that can be counterproductive when markets are volatile, because it creates needless fear and anxiety.

One-Time Snapshot

So, what if you are the type who can barely find the checkbook, much less balance it? The type who "files" receipts in every possible nook and cranny? The type who wouldn't be caught dead with a calculator? Even if you're math-challenged, or not very organized, you still can't escape needing to understand your expenses if you want any hope of early retirement or financial independence. So how should you do it?

First, let me suggest trying Mint. It was designed for overscheduled, organizationally challenged, modern life. It might just work for you.

But, if not, you'll need to find space and allocate just an hour, or a few, of concentrated time to *snapshot* what it costs you to live. If you really just want a quick answer, and not a tracking system, then you can perform a detailed analysis by hand. But, if at all possible, use an electronic spreadsheet like Excel to do the math. Here's how it works:

1. Gather all your bank statements, credit card statements, and miscellaneous bills together for the most recent full month.

2. Make a list of all possible spending categories (see below for ideas).

3. Work through every amount that you paid out for the month, tallying spending in each category.

4. Estimate the impact of annual expenses not reflected in the month's total: add in 1/12th of your annual property taxes, for example.

5. Add or subtract in categories to estimate how this spending could change once you're financially independent: subtract commuting expenses, and add travel expenses, for example.

If even this one-time manual approach seems overwhelming to you, then there is another way which is even quicker and easier:

1. Write down how much you earned last year. (Use your income tax return or final pay stub for the year.)

2. Subtract taxes you paid. (This rough approach assumes you'll be in a much lower tax bracket after retiring.)

3. Subtract any amounts you saved. (Find this on your year-end banking and brokerage statements, if possible.)

4. Subtract any debt you paid off, like old credit card balances.

5. The balance is the amount of money you spent on routine living expenses last year. Adjust for any remaining debt, and possible lifestyle changes in retirement, then divide by 12, to get a monthly budget.

The disadvantage of this last method is that it won't be terribly accurate. You may miss or over-count some large expenses. And, while you'll get some feel for how much money must be spent to maintain your lifestyle, you won't get information on exactly *where* that money is going – which makes it difficult to implement changes to accelerate your retirement.

And the disadvantage of any of these "snapshot" approaches is that you won't have an automated system in place once you're done that could give you continuous feedback on changes you make in your spending, or on changes in your lifestyle, over time. Nevertheless, you'll have more information and a better picture than if you did nothing. So I encourage you to take at least this *snapshot* of your finances, if nothing else.

2. "Budgeting"

Now that we've reviewed the need to be aware of your living expenses, plus several approaches for tracking those expenses, let's examine the concept of a *budget*. The dictionary defines a budget as "an itemized summary of estimated or intended expenditures for a given period." That sounds harmless enough, yet the word conjures up fear and loathing at work and home. Typical budgets require some math and discipline, which makes them about as appealing as a root canal for most people. In fact, some personal finance experts boldly proclaim that "budgets don't work!" But why not?

The reasons are more psychological and practical than financial. We all hate feeling restricted in our personal lives. We break budgets for the same reason we break diets: It requires too much organization and discipline ("willpower"). And the problem isn't entirely with *us*. Budgets are notoriously inflexible. Life doesn't play out into neatly organized categories that require the same outlay of resources each month. In practice, one category *gives*, while another *takes*.

But I have noticed that your overall monthly total expenses will likely remain steady, or within a certain range, over long periods of time. And that points us to the first of two crucial functions that a budget provides:

1. It tells you how much you need to live on a monthly basis so you can calculate income needs for financial independence or retirement.

2. And it indicates areas where you can cut back.

That's the real point of a budget. In my opinion, 90% of the value lies in the actual spending data, and only 10% in your stated goals. *Awareness* is key. My approach is to track spending carefully, understand what it costs you to live each month in all important categories, and keep in mind your goal to live below your means. The rest will happen naturally, without draconian adherence to an artificial "budget."

Categories

Central to any budgeting effort is a list of spending categories. The ideal list and organization will be a personal matter. It doesn't make sense to track categories that are too small to be meaningful or too large to be actionable. Aim for categories that constitute at least 1% of your monthly outlay, and no more than about 15%, if possible.

Thus, the exact categories will vary a bit from person to person. Try to create categories that isolate areas where you might be able to optimize spending. For example, don't combine dining out with groceries, just because it's all "food." Give recurring expenses, like utilities, a separate category too. It is important to watch that these don't ratchet up over time. Lastly, don't forget those less-frequent expenses such as home and auto repairs, vacations, and property taxes!

Until you form your own preferences, here is a list of categories and subcategories you can use to begin:

Auto: Loan/Lease

Auto: Insurance

Auto: Gas

Auto: Maintenance

Food: Groceries

Food: Dining Out

Gifts: Donations

Gifts: Personal

Health: Insurance

Health: Copays

Health: Prescriptions

Home: Mortgage/Rent

Home: Insurance

Home: Maintenance

Insurance: Disability

Insurance: Life

Insurance: Umbrella

Miscellaneous/Other

Personal: Care

Personal: Children

Personal: Clothing

Recreation: Entertainment

Recreation: Hobbies

Recreation: Travel

Taxes: Income

Taxes: Property

Utilities: Electricity

Utilities: Gas/Oil

Utilities: Phone/Internet/Cable

Utilities: Water/Sewer

Example

Any personal finance software like Quicken or Mint will be able to summarize your expenses into categories for you to review on a monthly basis, and create a budget, if you wish. Most likely, the default view will be all you need. However, in my case, I like to see a version of our budget that is organized and summarized a bit differently, so I transfer the numbers into a spreadsheet after each month ends. This takes only about 20 minutes, and provides me with a good opportunity to review our recent spending.

Whatever way you do it, take a bit of time each month to compare your *spending* to your *income*, and make adjustments as necessary to achieve your savings goals – which we'll discuss in more detail later. Look for the few categories where you could cut spending dramatically. You may find there are only one or two categories that you really need to watch carefully.

My budget spreadsheet features a list of categories as rows, with the targeted budget amount in the first column. The actual average amount spent for the current calendar year is in the next column. Then there is the percent of the total spending in the following column, so I can see, for example, that auto gas has consumed 9% of our budget in the last 12 months. (Graphing your expenses by percent in a pie chart can provide some eye-opening revelations about your money, and your priorities.) Finally, there are the actual detailed expenses compiled for each month. At the bottom are monthly totals. Here is an example:

Figure: Budget Summary

Category	Budget	Actual	%	May-11	Jun-11	Jul-11
auto - gas	$400	$411	9%	$136	$318	$499
auto - other	$150	$64	1%	$13	$40	$0
...	...	...	...	...	...	...
utilities - electric	$115	$102	2%	$90	$114	$111
utilities - gas	$85	$85	2%	$57	$42	$26
utilities - phone	$198	$240	6%	$226	$228	$202
utilities - water/sewer	$55	$40	1%	$122	$0	$0
TOTAL	$4,323	$4,356	100%	$4,503	$3,878	$5,652

3. Dealing with Debt

I've avoided debt like an affliction my entire life and so I claim no special expertise in how to reduce it or eliminate it. As with many modern lifestyle diseases, you are far better off avoiding the causes in the first place. If you have substantial debt, then it is probably too early to be thinking of financial independence or retirement, other than in a general way. Your focus should be on eliminating the debt.

Adding debt removes future choices. Most of the time, it represents borrowing from the future to embellish today. You'll come out far ahead in the long run by avoiding interest payments. Shun debt: It's hard to make progress on your long-term financial goals with debt still in the picture.

In theory, you can take on debt for things that might appreciate in value, like a home or an education. That would be a form of investing leverage. But nearly all such "assets" have become suspect in the modern world. We've experienced a historic housing bubble where millions of people paid top dollar for houses that may not appreciate in value for decades, if ever. And the cost of college education has been running ahead of inflation for years, while the benefits – salaries – continue to stagnate, except for some specialized or technical degrees.

You may have to take on debt to buy your first car. But try buying that vehicle used, and paying it off as quickly as possible. If you focus on saving and paying off debt quickly, then you will eventually build assets so that you will never again need to take out a loan. (We've had no car loans since the first decade of our marriage, long ago.)

If you do have debt, the most effective technique I know for getting rid of it leverages your own debt payments to pay off the obligation more quickly. Here is the essence:

1. Rank your debts in importance by interest rate.

2. Pay off the most critical (highest interest rate) debts first, while making minimum payments on the others.

3. Then apply the payments from those paid-off debts to your remaining debt.

Although, if you have several very small debts, you might build momentum fastest by paying them off first, regardless of the interest rate. At any rate, when you have debt, you should not take on extra spending obligations while any debt remains. Use every available cent to break the bonds of debt.

4. Evaluating Your Savings

While the first step to financial independence is becoming aware of, and taking control of, your expenses, *tracking your savings* follows shortly after. You will almost inevitably produce those savings once you become more aware of your expenses. And it's the steady growth in savings over time that will eventually produce the wealth you need to retire. So monitoring your savings is critically important. Just because it may grow slowly at times, don't make the mistake of ignoring it.

Now is the time to inventory all your accounts – checking, savings, investment, retirement – to make sure you have a handle on your assets. Ideally you'll realize you have more than you thought, when you see it all in one place. Or, you may find old accounts that just clutter your life – even worse if they have fees associated with them. As you begin to bring your financial life into focus, it's an excellent opportunity to consolidate accounts and financial institutions so you can concentrate your focus. Cash sitting in seldom-used accounts can often be put to much better use paying down debt or working in the stock market. And every individual account you must maintain is a potential source of distraction and expense that can detract from your ultimate goal of saving for an earlier retirement.

The most important account to fully assess and understand is your retirement plan or pension plan (for the few who have them), at work. It's shocking how little some employees know or understand about what will be the main source of wealth for the latter portion of their lives. Take an interest in your financial future and monitor your retirement account balance regularly. Understand what it's invested in. Evaluate the options for safer and cheaper investments. Understand what, if anything, your employer offers in matching funds, and how you can maximize getting them.

When you're done reviewing your retirement plan, give some thought to any unconventional or forgotten forms of savings you may possess. Were you gifted government savings bonds as a child? Do you own jewelry, or family heirlooms, or collectibles that ought to figure in your wealth? Are you on a joint account that you'll inherit from a parent? Do you have certificates or statements in a safe deposit box at the bank?

Finally, this is an opportunity to think about the unrealized *human capital* in your personal portfolio. Are you close to finishing a valuable degree or professional training? Do you have skills or hobbies that could produce a profit if developed? Though it's difficult, and probably not advisable, to assign an actual monetary value to these intangibles, thinking about them in the context of your savings, may motivate you to take the remaining steps to develop their worth. Producing more income through career advancement or starting a business on the side is a powerful way to accelerate your savings, and will be the subject of a later chapter in this book.

5. The Bottom Line: Your Net Worth

So far we've discussed tracking your spending and your savings. These two factors interact with a third – your income – to determine your financial future. In a nutshell, income that you don't spend is added to your savings. And your savings plus other significant assets that you own make up your *net worth* – your total wealth available to produce income and thus financial freedom.

Net worth is the single most important *indicator* for measuring, monitoring, and actually achieving financial success. This single number, computed and monitored regularly, has the power to tell you if you're headed in the right direction, whether you are becoming more or less financially independent.

Though the number itself must be interpreted with some care, like expenses, the simple act of monitoring it regularly may be most valuable of all. That teaches you, in simple and direct terms, whether your many financial activities – working, saving, borrowing, spending – are leading you toward financial freedom, or not. Simply put, *you need to spend less than you take in over time, and grow your savings*.

So, your net worth should *grow* in most years, which will indicate you are "living below your means." If it stays the *same*, and you are not yet financially independent, that means you aren't saving, and must plan on working indefinitely. If your net worth goes *down* for very long, you could be headed for a lifetime of indebtedness to others, or even bankruptcy.

Living below your means is *key* to accelerating retirement. Without that space between your income and your spending, you can't build the wealth that is required for financial independence.

Computing Net Worth

Since net worth is so important, let's jump right in and talk about how to compute it. Typically this calculation is known as a "Personal Balance Sheet." Net worth is defined as the amount by which your assets exceed your liabilities. So notice, for starters, there is little point in discussing net worth if you are in debt overall. Rather you need to focus on getting out of debt ASAP, then return for this discussion.

If you use a program such as Quicken, or a web tool such as Mint, then a calculated estimate of your net worth may be available via an easily accessible overview screen or report. I recommend making that view the default – so it's never far from your mind!

But it's also good to know how the software is computing that number, and to be able to do it yourself, which is easy enough....

Start by adding up the values of all your bank accounts (checking, savings), and any substantial cash you keep on hand. These are *assets*. Next, add in the current value of any and all investment accounts (update securities prices first, if needed, to reflect the latest stock market values). If you have retirement accounts that haven't already been considered, add them in too. If it's relatively early in your career and you have a defined benefit pension of some sort, add in the amount of your contributions, plus any vested employer contributions – the money you could take with you if you left your job. If you are married, then include the value of your spouse's similar accounts – you are actually computing your net worth together, as a couple.

Next, add in the value of your equity in significant personal property such as vehicles and houses. To start, you need a fair market value for those items. For vehicles, I use NADAguides.com. And for houses I use Yahoo.com or Zillow. com. Keep in mind that all such estimates are approximate, and tend to be optimistic, in my experience – perhaps because pessimistic values would bring less traffic to the web site! If you want to be conservative, shave 5-10% off the values from such sites. The only truly accurate price for personal property or real estate is found when you have a willing buyer with cash in hand.

If you don't owe anything on a house or vehicle, then you can simply add the fair market value to your net worth. But, if you have a mortgage or auto loan, then you need to subtract the outstanding balance on the loan (that's a *liability*) from the fair market value, to find your *equity* – the amount of the property that truly belongs to you, and not to the bank.

Finally, you need to subtract your liabilities, which are generally forms of debt, to arrive at your net worth. As a reminder, the following table lists various possible assets and liabilities, so you don't forget to count anything.

Summary Table: Computing Net Worth/Personal Balance Sheet

Assets (add)	Liabilities (subtract)
cash	credit card balances
checking	vehicle loans
savings	mortgages
CDs	home equity loans
investments	student loans
retirement: IRAs/401k's	consumer loans
pensions	personal debts
homes	
vehicles	
land	
businesses	
valuables/collectibles	
annuities	
life insurance policies	

Valuing Property

Note, while the equity in your home or vehicles *does* add to your net worth, and theoretically represents wealth that you can tap, it must be considered with caution. For one thing, property is not generally very liquid. The amount of cash it represents is inversely proportional to how eager you are to sell it. As many homeowners have discovered during recessions, the value of a home is much less than you might like, if you must sell it in a hurry.

Furthermore, property sales generally have high transaction costs, so some value will disappear in the process of transferring ownership. When transacting in real estate, for example, the buyer and seller, between them, must pay for appraisal fees, inspection fees, application fees, origination fees, points, commissions, title insurance, broker fees, recording fees, document fees, survey fees, and attorney fees.

Lastly, autos (if you must commute in one), and homes (if you still need to live in one), serve a valuable *function* in your life that must generally be replaced. So the money they represent is not available for producing other income. That money is part of your net worth, but it is not correct to consider it an "investment" for income-producing purposes, unless you rent the property, or a portion of it.

Given all these caveats about the value of property, it might not seem worth the bother to track it. But it *is* important to keep an eye on the equity in your property, because the expenses associated with property ownership can make or break your journey to financial independence.

For example, if the value of your home doesn't grow to offset the cost of mortgage interest, taxes, and maintenance – you'll be losing money. If you buy an expensive house or have one that grows greatly in value, you may be in a housing "bubble" with the subsequent risk of a crash and becoming "upside down" in your mortgage (owing more than your house is worth). For most of the 20th century, houses rarely depreciated, but now we know that they can.

Another problem: If your house represents a very large proportion of your net worth, it may be difficult or impossible to support your lifestyle without working indefinitely because all your wealth is wrapped up in an asset that doesn't produce income for you. This is known as being "house poor."

Unlike homes, new vehicles nearly always depreciate very quickly. Buying a new vehicle every few years will be a significant drag on your net worth over time. Used vehicles depreciate far more slowly. Thus tracking the value of your property year in and year out is essential, because it gives you an intuitive understanding and reminder of all these factors.

Other Difficult-to-Value Assets

Certain assets, such as pensions, businesses, personal debts, inheritances, annuities, and life insurance can be difficult to value, and may not necessarily make sense as part of your net worth. For pensions, your plan administrator should make available an estimate of benefits periodically, which can be used to calculate a present value. Small businesses are notoriously hard to value because of their lack of liquidity. Personal debts and inheritances must include some assessment of the risk of never being paid. And many annuity and life insurance products are frightfully complex and have obscure fees and penalties affecting their value.

In short, the certainty behind your net worth will decrease the more you own of these types of assets. Simplify your financial life as much as possible, then do your best to assign a value to what's left. Remember: The more complex or illiquid your assets, the more you'll be flying blind in your financial life, subject to the opinions of financial "experts," who may have motives of their own that conflict with your own best interests.

If you are in this situation and an asset is clearly beneficial, such as a business or a pension, then you may need to pay for an expert valuation, if that is important to you. If the asset is an emotional or logistical liability, like personal debt or some kinds of insurance policies, then you may be best served by liquidating it, and simplifying your life.

How Often?

Now that we've defined "net worth" and discussed *how* to compute it, let's consider *when*. You may be fortunate enough to already use personal accounting software or a web site that computes your net worth continuously. If not, you can easily set up a computerized spreadsheet, similar to the table above, that sums your assets and subtracts your liabilities.

How often should you update stock market prices and collect account balances to accurately compute your net worth? That's a matter of personal preference. I know of sophisticated investors who do it only *annually*, and others who do it much more frequently. *Daily* is too often: you'll be distracted by the "noise" of short-term stock market movements. And *weekly* is probably too often as well, unless the process is mostly automated.

For starters, I suggest you evaluate your net worth *quarterly*, and adjust the frequency from there to suit your disposition and needs.

Take Action

- If you do nothing else after reading this, resolve to institute some financial tracking at a level and frequency that's right for you. That's the most important first step to pilot your life to financial freedom. If you don't already have a software solution, then evaluate Quicken and Mint.com and choose one.

- Set up simple spending categories and take time each month to review your spending in each. Recognize and overcome any roadblocks to tracking your finances. Becoming aware of your expenses is essential to controlling them, and to budgeting for a financially independent lifestyle.

- Live below your means. The ability to spend less than you take in, whether you are a college student or a millionaire, is a fundamental behavior of all those who become financially independent.

- Get out of debt. You simply can't build wealth while you're accumulating its opposite: debt. You can't get to the top of the mountain if you're in a hole, and digging it deeper. Getting out of debt, if you have any, must be one of your top priorities on the path to financial freedom.

- Remember your single most important metric for

financial independence: your net worth. It's relatively easy to compute and, when tracked over time, it reveals a wealth of information about your financial situation.

- So, if you haven't already, sit down today and total up all your personal assets and liabilities. Take a few extra minutes to enter that data on your computer, and you'll have a valuable tool that will pay you priceless dividends in self knowledge over the years.

PART TWO: UNDERSTANDING YOUR RETIREMENT

"A man is rich in proportion to the number of things he can afford to let alone." — Henry David Thoreau

"The idea is to build a life so fulfilling that you never want to retire from it." — Todd Tresidder

This book will help you to accelerate your retirement. But there is little point in accelerating a journey until you know where you're going. Otherwise you risk overshooting, or arriving at the wrong destination!

This section addresses how to define your vision of retirement, so you'll know what it takes to get there, and so you can arrive either on, or ahead of, schedule. Also, by thinking ahead, you may be able to visualize and design a more *modest* version of retirement that still satisfies you. Then you'll be able to retire that much sooner!

We'll begin by exploring the concept of "retirement" and what it means to you. Defining your desired retirement lifestyle will let us assess approximately how much money you may need to retire safely and comfortably.

Then we'll briefly review some of the sources for the income you'll need in retirement. Finally, we'll dig into one of the primary threats to both retiring sooner and your ultimate retirement lifestyle – *inflation* – and the surprising control you have over your *personal* inflation rate, as proven by myself and other retirees.

6. What Do We Mean by "Retirement"?

The idea of *retirement* is an invention of the last century. Before then, people had no expectation of "retirement" in the modern sense.

So it's worth analyzing this concept a little more closely, before you arrive there, to make sure it's a place you want to go. What is the purpose and meaning of "retirement" to you? For me it wasn't about playing golf or lying on the beach all day. Retirement for me meant financial *freedom*, the ability to set my own itinerary and schedule, doing *what* I want, *when* I want, even though it sometimes resembles that four-letter word "work."

For most early retirees, retirement is an opportunity to be creative and productive on their own terms, to live life at their own speed. Specifically, it means you have *enough financial independence that you don't need to be tied to a full-time job.*

But virtually every bit of the mainstream financial infrastructure – media, brokers, advisors, retirement plans, tax laws, and regulations – is oriented towards seeing you work and work, until a conventional retirement age in your 60's. If you love your job and it makes the world a better place, why not? But if your job isn't meaningful to you, or if it's only a means to consumption of more stuff, then maybe early "semi-retirement" is an answer.

The true objective of "retirement," for me, was an *ideal work-life balance*. I talk and write about "early retirement" because it's a popular and easily grasped term. But, when you look at the numbers, and the futility of predicting future economic events, it's difficult, and not all that beneficial, to design a life with *no* work at all. For me, retirement is more about financial independence and choosing my own work. And I was willing to live modestly plus make some sacrifices to reach that point!

7. Your Retirement Lifestyle

I've discussed my own retirement philosophy a bit. Now it's your turn. What do you envision for the years when you no longer have to report to a full-time job? Where will you live and what will you do? Will you work part time, just for the fun of it, or to stay busy? Will you start a second career, perhaps one that is more about passion or service, and less about money? Will you travel much, or will some combination of old and new hobbies or pursuits occupy your time? Will you keep your current lifestyle, expand it, or reduce it a little, or a lot? Will you relocate or downsize to control expenses, or for a change of scenery?

It's important to ponder how you will spend your time and money in retirement because this will impact both your expenses and your required income. Even though you will be freed from full-time work, you won't be freed from the need to monitor and understand your expenses. And, even though work is no longer a prime necessity, you may find that you want a little extra income here and there, and you may in fact produce some income unintentionally, as you pursue your various interests.

To help you visualize different retirement options, and to help us budget for them in the next section, I'm going to paint pictures for you of *three possible retirement lifestyles*. Keep in mind that these are composite pictures based on my personal experience and what I hear from fellow bloggers and readers.

None of these pictures will suit you precisely, but each of them will contain elements that may appeal to you, or push you in a different direction. Use them to develop and benchmark your own vision of retirement:

Ultra Early Retirement – This is about getting to retirement as quickly as possible. You leave work in your 30's or 40's after having saved aggressively and lived very frugally. You own a smaller house in a working-class neighborhood in a smaller city, or you rent an older apartment in a mid-size city, or you choose a small farm in a rural location. You grow or make some of your own food, buy in bulk, eat low on the food chain, and rarely eat out. You get by with bicycling and public transportation, perhaps maintaining a single older vehicle for longer trips. You provide most of your own recreation in the form of low-cost sports, music, books, and other free media. You rarely travel out of town and, when you do, you camp or stay with friends and family. You produce some extra income on the side by being handy or selling crafts.

Moderate Early Retirement – This is about finding a balance between the working years and early retirement. You leave work in your 50's after having saved prudently and lived carefully. You live in a modest house in a nicer neighborhood, or downsize to a condo or small townhome. You shop for groceries carefully, buy less expensive generic items when possible, and eat out on a strict monthly budget. You maintain a couple of older vehicles, perhaps his and hers, or one compact and one larger for longer trips. You spend a few hundred dollars a month for recreation: sometimes it goes to purchasing luxuries, sometimes to events or gear. You spend the same on travel and travel regularly, usually just shorter trips. But you splurge on a few longer domestic trips each year that may involve flying and renting. You start a lifestyle business that showcases your creativity and may produce some income.

Plush Traditional Retirement – This is about maximizing your retirement comfort, security, and unstructured time. You leave work in your 60's or later after having saved regularly and enjoyed the finer things in life. Keeping a beautiful home is important to you. You remain in your family home or trade to an upscale townhome. You might maintain a vacation home elsewhere. You shop at the best grocers, eat out several times a week, often at the best restaurants. You continue to drive larger or luxury vehicles that you maintained during your working years. Recreation is a major part of your retirement lifestyle. You may have pricier club memberships or hobbies. You travel frequently and to popular vacation destinations, sometimes overseas. You no longer concern yourself with producing income, though you are open to consulting in your old occupation occasionally, should the opportunity arise.

Note, I prefer the less expensive retirement options. They are easier to achieve, and easier on the planet. But reasonable people choose each of these paths. It's most important to understand that each of these retirement pictures carries its own distinctive price tag, so we'll explore that next….

8. Your Retirement Goal: How Much Will It Cost?

Now that we've painted three possible pictures of retirement, let's look at the price tags, to give you some context for understanding your own desires and possibilities. Once you understand the costs of these different options, you can begin to choose appropriate saving goals for your own individual situation, and also begin to understand how long it will take you to get there.

Despite the variations in individuals, regions, and a host of other personal factors, it is possible to offer some broad cost-of-living numbers for different retirement lifestyles. The monthly expense numbers below are based on my own personal experience, before and during retirement, and that of hundreds of readers who have completed the reader survey on my web site. These represent both essential plus discretionary expenses for a couple living in retirement, assuming that your home or residence is already paid for.

In short, here are approximate costs for the various retirement lifestyle pictures:

Lifestyle	Monthly Expenses for Couple	Gross Retirement "Number"
Ultra Early	$2,000-$3,000	$750,000
Moderate Early	$4,000-$5,000	$1,350,000
Plush Traditional	$6,000+	$2,000,000+

Note, the retirement "number" above is the total amount of income-producing assets you must save over the course of your career in order to pay for the associated lifestyle. Usually that is *less than* your net worth, which will include real estate and personal property.

Also note that you may not need to save quite as much as shown above because you can add to your savings the value of pensions or Social Security benefits that you've accrued. I cover how to perform that calculation in my other writings on *CanIRetireYet.com,* and in my second book. In early to mid-career, the details are not critical or particularly ascertainable. But if you figure that Social Security will supply about *one-quarter* of your required savings, that's a reasonable, conservative guess that will suffice until you are closer to retirement.

The "Safe Withdrawal Rate"

How exactly did I compute the gross retirement "number" above? In this case, I used a 4% *safe withdrawal rate.* That rate is the outcome of numerous early academic studies showing that you can withdraw about 4% from your assets in the first year of retirement, while adjusting that amount for inflation in subsequent years, with a relatively low risk of running out of money over a 30-year retirement. (Note: To find the lump sum that can support a 4% annual withdrawal, multiply that annual withdrawal by a factor of 25. That works because the inverse of 4% produces a 25x multiplier. And that's why you'll often hear the rule of thumb that you must save "25 times your annual expenses" to retire.)

Unfortunately, that simple old rule of thumb is under considerable challenge now in current research. It turns out that the amount of money you need varies with the economic conditions in which you retire, and is not entirely predictable in advance. Your actual safe withdrawal rate could be as low as 3% or lower under poor economic conditions such as low interest rates and below-average stock market returns, and it could range as high as 5% or higher under some ideal conditions.

Given these uncertainties, and considering this book is focused on *accelerating* your retirement, not detailed *planning* for it, I will offer my own simple rule for your retirement number based on my reading of the latest wave of research:

> *If you are retiring with no ability or interest to ever work again, then plan on a 3% withdrawal rate (a 33x multiplier) for a high degree of safety. But if you are retiring with some flexibility – the ability to work part time or cut expenses to shore up your finances if the worst economic scenarios come to pass – then it's acceptable to plan based on a 4% withdrawal rate.*

My bottom-line advice is to acquire enough financial assets to ensure your baseline living essentials indefinitely, then ask yourself: "Am I doing what I love?" If not, leave behind your full-time career and "work" instead at what gives you meaning, with an eye on producing some income from it….

Computing *Your* Retirement Number

Given the general advice above, how should you go about deciding on your *own* retirement number? For a simple and relatively conservative answer, I'd follow these steps:

1. Assess your expenses and compute a monthly budget.

2. Multiply that monthly budget by 12 to get an annual budget.

3. If you envision a flexible, early retirement with the potential for some working income, multiply that number by 25.

4. Or, if you envision a more traditional retirement with fixed expenses and no potential for work, multiply that number by 33.

5. If you will pay into Social Security for your entire career, you can then reduce that number by 25% (multiply it by 0.75).

6. Use this final number as a *savings target*, but continue learning and refining it as you approach the actual retirement decision.

Disclaimer: This has been a general, broad-brush approach to the retirement question, intended to calibrate your expectations, and guide your savings efforts into the right ballpark for accelerating your financial independence. For more precise numbers in your personal situation, including how to assess pensions and Social Security, see my other writings at *CanIRetireYet.com*, my second book, or a financial planner.

9. Where Will the Money Come From?

It's generally very difficult to reach your retirement "number" with money from just one source. You will likely need to integrate multiple income streams to provide for a comfortable retirement.

Here are the most prominent sources for those income streams:

Your Savings – For many of us, our personal savings, in tax-sheltered retirement or taxable accounts, will be the largest source of retirement income, and the one over which we have the most control. How does a lump sum of savings turn into an income stream for life? That's one of the most difficult questions in retirement planning. In brief, there are two options: manage withdrawals from those assets yourself using a "safe withdrawal rate" or some other system, or hand those assets over to an insurance company in exchange for an annuity that pays you a guaranteed lifetime income.

Social Security – According to the U.S. Social Security Administration, 94% of all workers are covered under Social Security, and Social Security benefits represent about 39% of the income of the elderly. Social Security is a hugely popular and essential government program that, despite some tweaks in payroll taxes and benefit payouts, is likely to be around for the long haul. Chances are, you will receive some Social Security benefits, and that you will need them.

Pensions – Fewer and fewer American workers are covered by any sort of pension. Nearly 90% of the 1,000 largest companies in the U.S. have exited the retirement business, handing the issue off to employees through defined contribution plans such as 401k's. If you can count on any kind of pension, count yourself very fortunate.

Your Home – As an enforced pool of long-term savings, home equity is the largest source of wealth for many retirees. Whether that wealth represents rent-free shelter in retirement, or must be tapped for actual living expenses via equity loans or a reverse mortgage, the equity in your home is an important source of wealth, and potentially of retirement income.

Part-Time Work – Though traditional retirement excluded work, modern retirements with longer life spans and uncertain economic conditions will be much more likely to include some form of at least part-time work. Many of us *want* to continue being productive, though on our own terms, long into our golden years. And others will simply not have a choice, due to lack of saving, or high health care costs, and will need to keep working in some form.

Inheritance – An inheritance from parents *may* form part of your retirement income stream, but it would not be wise to count on it. Due to increasing life expectancies, rising medical costs, market volatility, and lack of savings, the average retiree going forward will probably inherit less, and later, than expected. Various studies report median inheritances for boomer households in the 5-digit range: nice to have, but not the kind of money that can singlehandedly finance a retirement, much less an early one.

Now that we've reviewed your retirement lifestyle, its expenses, and the income required, let's explore one important way your expenses could change over time….

10. Your Personal Rate of Inflation

Inflation is often seen as the termite of the financial world. Gnawing away at your assets over long periods of time, it's said to be an insidious threat. Hard to detect over short time frames, it could seriously damage your assets in retirement, robbing your portfolio of much of its growth, and crippling your purchasing power.

For much of the last decade, a chorus of voices have pointed out the dangers of inflation, and warned that the Fed's current policy makes it all but inevitable. I loathe the idea of politicians undermining our money supply as much as anyone. But are we actually seeing that? My personal expense data doesn't exactly show it.

Anybody planning to live in retirement without a salary for decades will encounter dire predictions for inflation. But how does inflation impact *your lifestyle*? Could you have a personal inflation rate that is quite different from the government's figures?

Official Measures of Inflation

First some definitions: Inflation is the percentage rate at which prices for goods and services in an economy *increase*. If the inflation rate is 3%, then something that costs $100 now, will cost $103 next year, $106.09 the following year, and $109.27 the year after that. Just like a savings account in reverse, the effects of inflation compound over time – not a good thing.

The government uses several different measures for inflation, which may or may not relate well to your personal experience. The most familiar measure is the Bureau of Labor Statistics (BLS) "headline" Consumer Price Index (CPI or CPI-U), which is a measure of the average change in prices paid by an urban consumer for a certain "basket" of goods and services.

The CPI market basket is drawn from eight areas: food, housing, apparel, transportation, medical care, recreation, education, and other. Because the CPI is weighted by the amount of income a typical consumer spends in each area, it also constitutes a *cost of living index*. But that doesn't mean it represents *your* cost of living, necessarily!

Another interesting measure of inflation from the BLS is the Chained Consumer Price Index (C-CPI-U). This index, which was published beginning in 2002, uses a formula to take into account consumers' *changing behavior in the face of rising prices*. Because, on average, when the price of some food item goes through the roof, we don't continue spending blindly on it. Instead, we substitute.

Perhaps because it is newer, or because it is less beneficial to most constituents, the C-CPI-U is not yet widely used in government programs. The difference in CPI-U and C-CPI-U has only averaged about 0.3 to 0.4% in some recent years, indicating that the *average* consumer has limited room to adjust his or her lifestyle in the face of price increases. But you don't have to be an average consumer....

My Experience with Inflation

Beginning in 1989, I've recorded virtually every dollar we spent in Quicken. I can easily review transactions from decades ago. What I see is not exactly what you'd expect from listening to the mainstream media's fears regarding inflation....

Nice meals out used to cost $30-$40. Nowadays those same meals might be $40-$50. We were paying $20 to fill up our cars back then – about what we pay now to fill up our Prius hybrid. An oil change was about $30. Still is. I paid $180 for a CD boom box. Now you can get one for a third of that. New music CD's were costing $15 apiece, now they're usually several dollars less. I bought a pair of pants and a new suit. The prices looked about the same as what I'd expect to pay today.

So what gives? On the face of it, the cost of living more than two decades ago doesn't look all that different than it does today. One area was a bit more expensive, a number of areas look about the same, and some areas – notably electronics – are actually *significantly cheaper now*.

But, according to the Bureau of Labor Statistics Inflation Calculator, $1 in 1989 should be worth about $1.87 in 2013. The average inflation over that time period was about 2.8% annually. Put another way, a 2013 dollar should be worth only about 53% of what it was in 1989. Yet, for a random sampling of my purchases, that just isn't so. What gives?

Government measures of inflation are likely to impact

your income from various government programs. But when it comes to your *personal budget* – spending to live comfortably in retirement – your *personal* rate of inflation is far more important. And, in my experience, this is quite different from the government's figures.

Just one reason that your personal rate of inflation could be different from the CPI is that the government weights prices according to the priorities of the average consumer. If your consumption patterns are different, your weights will be different. For example the CPI weights housing costs at about 40% of living expenses. If you own your home, or rent a modest place, you may not spend that much on housing.

Another reason your experience may vary is geographical. Different regions of the country will experience different rates of inflation, especially for housing, food, and fuel. If you retire in a low-cost area, you can easily beat the national CPI.

Yet another reason for variation is your level of thriftiness, and the timing of your purchases. If you are frugal, hunt for bargains, and buy used, on sale, and out of season – you may not experience the same inflation rate as the average consumer.

For example, grocery costs are one area where our personal inflation rate has defied official figures. Surely our food costs have gone up in the past two decades? Well, it's hard for me to normalize our early data because it starts just as we were starting a family. But I *can* say that our grocery expenses have gone *down* by hundreds of dollars a month in recent years....

Why? Well, the first big leg down was when we became

empty nesters. But we accomplished another big leg down, just the two of us, by re-focusing on careful shopping and pantry management, and economical, mostly meat-free meals. The end result? We've reduced our grocery budget by more than 20% over the last 3 years! So we've engineered our own personal "deflation."

Your Secret Weapons Against Inflation

So there are a variety of reasons for variations between your personal rate of inflation and that of the average consumer. Obviously, for us, inflation hasn't been as severe a problem in at least some categories of spending as the government and pundits would have you believe. There are two main factors:

1. Those of us accustomed to living frugally are sensitive to higher prices, and practiced at modifying our lifestyles to deal with them. Instead of paying twice as much for a certain food, we'll simply adjust our diet. Instead of paying high prices for gas, we'll live closer to work and drive more fuel-efficient vehicles. Instead of supersizing into fancier houses and cars, we'll downsize. So even the official Chained CPI for the average consumer understates the ability some of us have to adapt.

2. Technology and productivity growth have kept a lid on inflation, even reversed it, in areas such as electronics. But the impact on other goods and services of new efficiencies and quality standards has been widespread also. To the extent you can keep

your consumption constant, instead of increasing it along with what's offered in the marketplace, your cost of living could be stable over time. For example, technology has driven the cost of video displays relentlessly down, but the average consumer response has been to buy more and bigger displays. The same pattern is visible in housing, transportation, and other areas. We hear about how cheap cars or houses were for our parents or grandparents decades ago. Yet today's cars last longer, and today's houses tend to be larger – so those comparisons may be suspect.

In the end, scrutinizing and optimizing your lifestyle will pay greater dividends than the general wisdom about inflation allows. Prices do increase in some areas that we can't control. (Health care comes to mind.) But in many other areas, inflation can be muted over even several-decade time spans, because technology plus our own behavior give us wide latitude to control it effectively.

Retirement and Your Personal Rate of Inflation

Understanding and monitoring your personal rate of inflation is crucial to the success of your retirement, and to the savings program that will make that retirement possible for you. Every percentage point of inflation that you accept into your lifestyle – whether it is genuine baseline inflation in the value of the dollar, or whether it is "lifestyle" inflation where you accept society's wants as your new needs – undermines your financial independence. Simple behaviors like shrewd, flexible shopping and not buying the latest consumer technology immediately can have profound impacts on your financial success.

On one level, inflation determines the increase in both your pre-retirement and retirement budgets over time. Thus it dictates your living expenses, and how much money you must save. On another level, inflation robs your investments of their earnings power, reducing their *real* return (the return in addition to inflation). For a typical 30-year career, or a 30-year retirement, if you can shave just 1% off the official inflation rate, it could mean tens of thousands of dollars, and years of work, saved.

Bottom line: *You don't have to accept the official inflation rate!* This understanding of inflation's role in your retirement and financial independence is unique, and is validated by my experience. It gives you a huge advantage over conventional retirement planning that mindlessly accepts inflation and spending as parameters over which you have no control. And this approach to inflation is part of why I was able to retire early. Not because I ignore or minimize the effects of inflation going forward (I don't), but because by *controlling* personal inflation in the decades leading up to my retirement, I was able to save so much more!

Take Action

- Predicting how much your retirement will cost requires understanding what "retirement" means to you, and what kind of retired lifestyle you want. So visualize your future living situation, what you'll do for recreation, and how you'll remain productive and creative.

- Taking a hard look at your lifestyle now, think about how it will change, or remain the same, once you reach financial independence. Adopt a modest lifestyle as soon as possible, so you can acclimate to it, and save even more towards early retirement.

- Figuring your ballpark retirement "number" will help you calibrate the tradeoffs needed to reach financial independence sooner. If you're a long ways off, you may want to make radical changes. If you're on schedule, you may want to focus on consistency.

- Understanding the various kinds of retirement savings and income, will help you to be realistic about the sources of retirement wealth, and let you plan for your retirement lifestyle.

- Tracking your expenses, and comparing them over time, will let you understand and control your personal rate of inflation. Not only can this reduce your current expenses, but it gives you valuable leverage over cost of living increases in the future. Being aware of the differences between official rates of inflation, and your personal rate, will help you control your lifestyle, free you from ordinary consumption patterns, and let you retire even sooner.

PART THREE: TOOLS FOR ACHIEVING FINANCIAL INDEPENDENCE

"He who pursues learning will increase every day." — Lao-Tzu

"Keep it simple: as simple as possible, but no simpler." — Albert Einstein

When analyzing ways to accelerate your retirement, the options generally fall into three categories: (1) increasing income, (2) decreasing expenses, or (3) optimizing how you manage your money. To reach retirement quicker, you will want to leverage all three.

Of these three options, increasing income is generally the most flexible option, and decreasing expenses the most common. We'll cover both of those important options in the last section of the book. But option (3), optimizing money management, is the easiest and least painful option. And we'll cover that option here.

If you can avoid blunders and reduce unnecessary expenses in managing your nest egg, you can shave years off your time to retirement. And managing your money yourself, as opposed to hiring an advisor, is the surer route to retiring sooner. Ultimately, if you want to retire early, you simply can't afford the expense and overhead of most investment professionals.

The U.S. has created a patchwork retirement system supplemented by the financial services industry. Most of us will be required to construct our own retirement plans using a few essential services from that industry, while sifting through mounds of dubious, conflicting, and usually expensive extras.

In the pages that follow I'll give you essential advice from my own experience on how to navigate the range of available financial services, choosing only what you need. These are the key tools for building wealth faster, and retiring sooner.

11. Saving: Just Do It

The first, second, and third thing to know about saving is *just do it*. Squirrel away as much of your income as you can. As long as you don't do crazy things with that money like buy collectibles or put it all in your brother-in-law's new business scheme, your savings *rate* – the amount you save compared to your income – will be far more important in the early years than exactly *where* you put that savings.

The best way to ensure you are saving consistently is to make it *automatic*. Be sure to opt in for payroll deductions, preferably the maximum, to fund retirement accounts such as 401k's and IRAs. Then, if possible, save even *more* by setting up an automatic monthly transfer from the account where your paycheck is deposited to a savings or investment account.

When you have a little free cash, get in the habit of using it to add to your investments or pay down debt, including mortgage debt. These are all forms of saving and, if you make them habitual over time, they will result in your retiring years earlier.

One of the most important steps you can take over the long haul is to *save raises and bonuses* rather than ratcheting up your lifestyle to spend them. As I write this, we've lived in the same house now for more than 16 years, which is actually *smaller* than the house we lived in before that. After having achieved a certain baseline of comfort, you can be very happy in your current lifestyle. So why increase it just because you have more money at hand? When you get a raise or bonus, I suggest splurging on an appropriate *one-time* expense with a small portion of it, and saving the rest, rather than taking on an increased mortgage, car payment, memberships, or other services that commit you to an expanded, and more expensive, lifestyle – *permanently*.

It's especially helpful to develop a mindset that values and takes satisfaction in saving. I would picture myself literally buying physical bank shares or shares of stock when I made a deposit or investment. And that feeling was reinforced when I reviewed the growing numbers on my financial statements each month. However you do it, the point is to teach yourself to take as much satisfaction in saving as you would in buying physical possessions. And, of course, that saving will do much more for your financial position over the long run.

Next, ensure there is a plan for growing your money. Don't leave your wealth unattended for years when it could be hard at work for you. The following chapters will show you how.

12. Savings Vehicles

A primary rule of retiring early is to *live below your means*. That means you spend less than you take in. An unavoidable conclusion is that you'll have money left over. So what do you do with that? Where do you put it? We'll explore that next.

You must put your money somewhere. Under the mattress won't do, and the default choices pushed on you by your bank may not be suitable either. So here are some thoughts on the different possible destinations for your early retirement savings....

Cash

In general, cash is not your friend on the path to early retirement. I keep enough in my wallet to pay for an emergency car repair or a taxi ride to the nearest ATM or airport, but I never use it. I pay for a sub-$5 food or drink purchase once or twice a month, and otherwise I really don't need cash in my wallet. I suggest aggressively minimizing your own use of cash. In addition to being a theft target, it's hard to track, and a temptation to spend. And it's surely no mechanism for *accumulating* assets.

Note: There are some systems for managing credit and getting out of debt by first putting yourself on a strict cash diet. If that's what you require to get control of your credit cards, so be it. But, in the long run, you'll need to be able to manage credit (or debit) cards effectively, and minimize your use of cash, to build substantial wealth.

Checking Account

Though the era of hand-written paper checks is rapidly disappearing, everybody still needs a checking account. This is your high-volume, low interest-bearing account, for the bulk of your routine financial transactions. For starters, it's where your income, probably a paycheck, should go before being divided up.

A checking account is also the primary mechanism, along with your credit cards, for monitoring and controlling your monthly living expenses. To minimize effort and reduce errors, I strongly recommend *automating* all of your bill-paying through your checking or credit card accounts. (I no longer manually pay *any* routine bills.) The peace of mind that comes from knowing I will never miss a payment, or get hit with a late fee, is priceless. I also love knowing that I can be on the road for months, if I want, and my finances will run on autopilot.

However, as essential as a checking account may be, it still is *not* the place to accumulate assets. Not only will your savings earn very poor rates of return, if any, sitting in a checking account, but they will be too susceptible to being spent on impulse. I don't generally keep more than a few months of expenses in our checking account. If you're just starting out, are well organized, and are counting every penny, then you may want to keep only a *single* month's expenses in a checking account, so the rest of your short-term savings can be earning interest elsewhere.

Savings and Money Market Accounts

The first place to turn once you've accumulated more than a few months of expenses in a checking account, is a linked savings or money market account. The reason is simple: Those accounts will pay more interest and, by being linked to your checking, preferably with automatic overdraft protection, they will seamlessly back up your monthly bill paying, if necessary. Savings and money market accounts are generally limited to six withdrawals per month, making them unsuitable for everyday transactions. And checking, savings, and money market deposit accounts are all FDIC insured (up to $250,000), which is the safest your short-term money can be in the world today.

Depending on your income, expenses, job security, time until retirement, and sensitivity to risk, I'd keep somewhere between 3 months and 2 years of living expenses in an easily accessible savings or money market account. If you are younger, 3-6 months is the conventional figure. If you are retired, 2 years will let you outlast most bear markets. This is the classic *emergency fund*. Its purpose is to float you between jobs, in your working years, and insulate you from being forced to sell other assets at a loss, in your retirement years.

Certificates of Deposit (CDs)

CDs are a popular mechanism for earning guaranteed rates of return that are somewhat larger than what you can expect on a savings account, in exchange for locking up your money at the bank for a set period. The compelling features of a CD are its guaranteed return and safety, but those come at a price. Be advised that most CDs come with substantial early withdrawal penalties – minimums set by federal law and maximums at the bank's discretion – that could even cause you to lose money in some cases. CDs are heavily marketed by banks and are probably very profitable for them.

I don't use CDs. I just have not found the risk/reward ratio very compelling for my own investing. A CD requires that you relinquish control of your money for a fixed period, which represents inflation and interest rate risk, and yet the total reward for doing that is often miniscule, unless very large sums are involved.

When I have sums of money that I don't need for a certain period, I'm more interested in higher-yielding investments such as dividend-paying stocks and short- or intermediate-term bonds. The two scenarios where I can possibly see using CDs would be (1) as an ultra-safe place to park money from the sale of one home that is designated for buying another home within a year or two, and (2) as rungs in a ladder for short-term retirement income, if interest rates are favorable and bonds aren't appropriate.

Your Home and Other Real Estate

Real estate is an extremely important savings vehicle for many, with home equity being the largest source of wealth for most savers. Paying down your mortgage is often one of the safest and surest investments you can make – giving a guaranteed return equal to the current interest rate on your mortgage.

But home improvements – especially expensive ones using luxury materials installed by a contractor and financed with borrowed money – are almost never "investments" or "savings" in my book. And such home improvement expenses no longer add to the value of your home dollar-for-dollar, if they ever did. According to MSN, the return on a remodeling investment has eroded from about 87% in 2005 to about 58% in 2012. On the other hand, modest, self-financed, do-it-yourself projects stand a much better chance of turning out to be profitable investments.

Defined Contribution Plans: 401k's, 403b's, etc.

An employer's defined contribution plan will be the next stop for most retirement savers. In addition to tax-sheltered growth, these plans have one other enormous savings advantage in most cases: *employer matching*. Depending on the specific benefits offered by your employer (the matching rate is up to them, within broad limits), this could supercharge your savings by 50% or more annually.

A key issue in employer-provided retirement plans remains the quality of your investment choices. Expensive, actively managed mutual funds are still too common in these plans, and shockingly expensive and complex annuities are all too common in the plans of some of those least able to afford them, such as public schoolteachers and safety workers.

Nevertheless, because payroll deduction can enforce a consistent saving habit, and because employer matching can enhance savings dramatically, you should almost always fully participate in any employer-sponsored plans for which you are eligible. And you should usually contribute the maximum to any such employer-provided plan each year, or at least enough to get all the matching funds your employer offers.

IRAs: Traditional and Roth

The next stop for retirement savings after maxing out employer plans is usually a Traditional or Roth IRA. These are self-administered retirement plans that grow tax-deferred. Their important differences include the tax treatment at the time you contribute and withdraw, and the required minimum distributions.

There is such a wealth of information available on IRAs that I'm not going to reiterate it all here. But I will make a couple points. **First**, there is an overwhelming tendency to favor Roth IRAs these days, and certainly they are a reasonable default choice, offering generally greater flexibility than Traditional IRAs. But be advised that so much of the pro-Roth advice, especially the advice to convert other retirement funds into a Roth, is predicated on the belief that tax rates will go *up* in retirement.

It's true, we are living in a changed economic world, where – all other things being equal – taxes are likely to go up, at least on the wealthy. But beware that, for many historically, the tax rate in retirement has gone *down*, because a retiree's income is usually substantially reduced. (And should your income *not* be reduced in retirement, maybe you don't need to fret so much about taxes.) Lacking a crystal ball for looking into the future, a good plan is to *diversify* your retirement savings across different types of retirement accounts, rather than assuming one certain scenario will play out in the future.

Second: Be careful about locking up your money exclusively in retirement accounts, if you are on track to *retire early*. If you are a high-wage earner who lives frugally and is focused on early retirement (before age *59½*), you must be careful not to *over save* in those retirement accounts, because you'll be penalized for any early withdrawals. If you retire much younger than is conventional, then you'll need to live for many years off your *taxable* accounts, before ever touching retirement accounts, and so you must divvy up your savings accordingly.

Brokerage Accounts

A brokerage account is usually composed of a linked checking or money market "sweep" account holding cash, plus any market holdings. This is the first step to investing in individual stocks and bonds – something I don't particularly recommend for most investors. But a brokerage account can also be a platform for buying mutual funds and ETFs (Exchange-Traded Funds) – which I do recommend.

However, you don't need a brokerage account to buy mutual funds: Vanguard, for example, as well as many other custodians, will let you buy them directly. So, while there is nothing wrong with opening a brokerage account, and it may give you access to a diversity of investment products, it is very likely an unnecessary step for many investors. For more on the specific custodians that I recommend, see the following chapters.

Note, your brokerage should pay you some nominal interest on cash holdings, though you'll probably have to manually move cash to a different type of account to get competitive rates.

Deferred Annuities

Annuities are the only available savings vehicles that can grow tax-deferred without having to exist inside an IRA or other retirement plan. This makes them potentially appealing as a last-resort destination for long-term savings that you want to grow sheltered from taxes. I say "last resort" because there are so many preferable savings vehicles to consider before taking on an annuity.

Annuities, especially variable annuities, are frightfully complex and often hide very high expenses that will have a greater impact on your savings than the supposed benefits and guarantees that the annuity contract itself provides.

Annuities generally only make financial sense for the relatively wealthy, under specific savings and taxation scenarios. If you fall into that group you probably know who you are and have the means to analyze the complexities of an annuity contract.

13. Custodians: Financial Services

Everyone must rely on some financial institution to hold their assets and execute their instructions in the market. And those institutions can be a reliable source of financial advice. So where should you turn first? There are just a few companies that I can personally recommend with confidence....

While there are other financial services companies with honorable management and good customer service, two rank above the rest in my book because their unique client-owned business structures all but guarantee that customers are rewarded first:

Vanguard is the United States' largest mutual fund company and home to its oldest balanced mutual fund. The management company at Vanguard is owned by Vanguard's mutual funds, and thus by those funds' shareholders who pay only what it costs to operate the funds. This structure eliminates any conflict of interest between investing clients and owners. They are one and the same. It also means that profits tend to flow to clients' benefit. Many Vanguard funds also incorporate penalties against short-term trading, paid to the fund. It all adds up to favorable incentives and lower costs for you, the client.

USAA is uniquely structured as an "insurance exchange" under state law. Clients or members, again, are like owners. Profits are retained or returned to members. USAA requires you to have some military connection in your family to join, and prides itself on operating with "military values." In my personal experience, this is more than just a slogan. The company thrived during the Great Recession because of its conservative investment policies. Customer service is also exceptional: USAA has won a number of J.D. Power customer service awards. I'm most familiar with their banking and insurance products, where costs have been competitive and service superior, in my experience.

There are two other for-profit companies that stand out to me:

Charles Schwab is a discount brokerage with a strong focus on customer value. They are inexpensive, and offer an excellent web site, and conservative, sensible analysis of the market. I've had an account with them for well over a decade. They've never surprised me with inappropriate fees, and, though they have their own investment products, they usually promote them in an accurate, low-pressure manner. Schwab offers a broad range of mutual funds with no loads or transaction fees. (Unfortunately you will have to pay a bit to buy Vanguard funds at Schwab.) Schwab also has offices in most sizable cities, where you can meet with a broker in person, if that is important to you.

Fidelity is a discount brokerage with a similar profile to Schwab. Though they are a 60-year-old company, they are privately owned, which means there is no shareholder pressure for short-term performance results. Fidelity has been ranked #1 for overall online broker by Kiplinger for two years running.

So those are four solid choices: Vanguard, USAA, Schwab, Fidelity. There are probably other trustworthy organizations out there. But these are the ones I can personally recommend. And I would definitely steer clear of most *banks*, particularly large national banks identified with Wall Street. In my experience, banks are expensive, rigid, overly conservative with your choices, and overly aggressive, behind the scenes, with your money.

14. Money Management: Doing It Yourself

A while back I analyzed threads on a popular retirement forum and found that the #1 topic was how to get accurate, impartial, and trustworthy financial *advice*. It's a big issue for everybody who needs to manage their money. Who do you listen to, and who can you trust?

I began serious investing in my mid-30's and retired, financially independent, at age 50. I never paid a financial advisor during that time, though there were various brokers assigned to my accounts. Occasionally, I'd have friendly conversations with them. But, by far, the most important instruction I received during all those years came from the *independent financial press* – individuals not employed by the major media or financial companies, and from my own trial and error.

Do *you* need a financial advisor? My answer for most people, most of the time, is "*NO - Manage your own money.*" Why? The primary reason to do it yourself is that nobody can care about your savings the way you can. You are the one who traded the days and years to earn it, and only you can truly understand what it's worth to you. And there are many other good reasons to do it yourself....

You will save money. The expense of an investment advisor can be considerable. Financial professionals are generally smart, aggressive, and capable individuals with significant business overhead. They can and do get paid very well – regardless of the results they produce. Meanwhile, you take on the risk. Their results are rarely predictable, and never guaranteed – but their fees are.

Some advisors charge a percent of assets under management. *The Wall Street Journal* reports that the average advisor's fee was about 1.3% in 2010, but the most expensive quartile of advisors charged nearly 2.1%. These may sound like small amounts, but compound those percentages over time with large sums of retirement savings and you're easily looking at tens of thousands of dollars in extra costs. Once in retirement, those fees can equate to *one-fourth* or *one-half* of all the income off your investments. That's like adding another mouth or two to feed in your home! You can save significant money by doing it yourself.

You are impartial. An advisor might be very nice, friendly, and honest – most are – but if they receive lucrative *commissions* by selling specific financial products, they simply cannot be impartial when recommending options to you. For example, beware of adopting an insurance agent or stock broker as your advisor. Usually, these folks make a living by selling financial products. They are in *sales*. Optimized, impartial advice is not their job.

Also, financial professionals are under a regulatory microscope that discourages free speech and creative thinking, encourages a conservative herd mentality, and further limits your options. You need accurate, impartial answers, with no agenda, not a one-size-fits-all solution that optimizes an advisor's profits.

You are committed. Then there is the question of time. Most advisors spend just a few hours each year, at best, with a given client. Only the most conscientious will monitor client portfolios on a regular basis, and even then probably only if you have a larger account. According to *AdvisorOne*, an industry publication, the average client-principal ratio at advisory firms is 140 to 1. According to *SmartMoney*, in a 2010 survey of more than 6,500 financial professionals, 66% said that *growing their business* was their top priority, while only 25% said that meeting more frequently with current clients was a top priority. My own informal experience confirms that most advisors are primarily concerned with finding new clients and selling better to them. You could spend just 30 minutes a week managing your own investments, and quickly be dedicating far more time to your account than a paid professional ever will!

For an organized individual with at least some interest in investing, I don't see merit in hiring an advisor to manage investments on a regular basis. That's a waste of money for most people. There is overwhelming evidence that the do-it-yourself passive index investing approach introduced below will beat an advisor in the majority of cases, especially an advisor who actively trades. Few advisors outperform the market, and none can guaranteed it. Even an advisor who makes use of the same funds as a do-it-yourselfer will likely underperform them, due to fees.

But even if you do manage your own money, you will need information and guidance from others, both at the start, while you are learning, and when you encounter complex financial decisions. Where should you go? Your first stop, in my opinion, should be independent voices with experience, those who have already accomplished what you want to do. That's one reason I'm writing here about my experience in retiring early. And why I recommend many other similar sources on the Resources page at CanIRetireYet.com.

15. Do You Need an Advisor?

But there are a handful of complex financial decisions, where you might want the help of an advisor. These include choosing an asset allocation, rebalancing, deciding when to take Social Security, valuing a pension, or evaluating annuity purchase options.

If you need an advisor, I strongly recommended finding one who charges a simple *hourly fee*. You don't want to pay *continually,* based on all of your assets, for tasks that are performed only *occasionally*.

Start by contacting one of the companies identified under "Custodians" earlier: Each has advisors who can offer individual financial advice, structured to minimize conflict of interest. But, even within those companies, you'll still need to identify a trustworthy and competent advisor. You've probably developed your own instincts for deciding who to trust with critical matters. I watch if somebody handles details in a professional and ethical manner.

How do you determine *competence*? Start with their years of experience. Have they managed money through at least one, preferably several, major downturns? How did they do? A look at an advisor's certifications may be helpful. The Certified Financial Planner (CFP) is the "gold standard" in personal finance certification. Anybody who passes the CFP exam is very bright and can crunch numbers. On the other hand, the CFP curriculum cannot always keep up with the latest in personal finance. So be advised, just because you are dealing with a CFP, doesn't make them an expert on your particular needs.

16. Passive Index Investing

Once you've accumulated significant assets, chosen savings vehicles and custodians, then decided where to go for advice, the question remains: How should your money actually be invested?

As I said in the introduction, this is not an investing book, and being a stock market wizard is not necessary to retire early. What *is* necessary is to use common sense, and avoid blunders. This can best be achieved by an investing strategy that features:

- Simplicity

- Diversification

- Low costs

- Patience

After more than two decades of study, trial, error, and lessons learned, I'm convinced this means *passive index investing*. In this style of investing you generally buy and hold just a few mutual funds or exchange-traded funds (ETFs) which in turn hold broad cross-sections of the bond and stock markets, at very low cost to you. Rather than actively trading, trying to guess and time the market's highs and lows, you hold the same few investments over very long time periods, which tends to even out volatility.

Most people, me included, don't have time to do a good

job – if that's even possible – of picking or actively trading individual stocks. There is a mountain of available evidence that passive index investing has the highest-probability of success for most investors. For example, Rick Ferri (a financial advisor and author of six investment books) reports that a portfolio of 5 passive index funds from different asset classes has a 90% chance of trumping a portfolio of 5 actively managed funds over 5 years. And, over a 20-year period, those odds jump to 98%!

Passive index investing was the second half of my own path to wealth (the first half was business ownership). I made some false starts early on: buying and selling the wrong things at the wrong times. But I was fortunate to find the guidance of a seasoned investing mentor while still in my 30's. And the one-two punch of a high savings rate from my engineering career plus diversified, low-cost, passive index investing with regular buying through market downturns, led to steady and substantial growth in our nest egg, and early financial independence.

For those with more money than time, those who work at high-paying careers and can be diligent and patient, passive index investing using low-cost mutual funds and ETFs, is the best choice for long-term wealth creation. That's my experience, and the experience of dozens of readers who have responded to the survey on *CanIRetireYet.com*. Most of us who have experimented with more aggressive approaches, have been burned, and then returned to passive index investing – the surest route to stock market wealth over the long haul.

Any of the previously mentioned custodians can walk you through the basics of passive index investing, help you choose an asset allocation, and select appropriate investments in less than an hour. In the simplest case, you can get started with just two funds: a broad *stock* fund, and a broad *bond* fund.

There is more that can be said on passive index investing and most of it has already been said, very well, in other places. (I'll recommend some additional resources at the end of this section.) But, just in case you're pressed for time, let me offer you a brief primer on two key components of investing: asset allocation and rebalancing....

Asset Allocation

Asset allocation – how you deploy your investments among major asset classes such as stocks, bonds, real estate, and cash – is a pillar of modern investing practice. Early studies found that much of your investing success or failure is due to asset allocation, as opposed to market timing or stock selection. Some later studies show asset allocation to be less critical. Nevertheless, it is the main choice you must make to get started investing, after you've chosen a custodian, so let's explore it a bit.

The asset allocation you choose will dictate both the volatility of your portfolio and the long-term returns you can expect from it. Typically these are inversely related, so the traditional approach to asset allocation attempts to assess your "risk tolerance." Everybody wants high returns, but not everybody can stomach the risk, or fluctuations, required on the way to those returns.

There are a myriad of risk-assessment tools in use. Most are dubious, in my opinion, because they ask you to imagine various critical scenarios and then guess at your feelings about them. I don't know about you, but my experience has been that it's completely impossible to know how you'll feel about most major life situations (think getting married, or raising children), until you are actually *in* them!

A common rule of thumb for asset allocation is to "put your age in bonds" (and cash). That rule has some merit, but assumes that young people are more risk tolerant and should own more stocks, which isn't necessarily so.

Given all this, what I will show you shortly is an asset allocation that begins in the "middle" – not entirely safe, but not very risky either. This also happens to be the allocation, more or less, that I've used for many years. It has produced solid returns, letting me retire early, yet never lost so much in a down market that I felt financially threatened. Since it starts in the middle, there is less likelihood of being far off the mark, and you can adjust it in small increments as you gather real-world experience.

Warning: Just because this allocation has served me well doesn't necessarily mean it's right for you. Your risk tolerance and goals are different from mine. You won't know your own goals without analyzing them, and you won't know your own true risk tolerance until you've lived through a market downturn or two. If you need professional advice to choose an asset allocation, seek out a professional advisor.

The more technically inclined or wealthy you are, the more asset classes you may choose to invest in. Here I will discuss the very basics, which are more than adequate for the majority of investors. The top three asset classes that everybody must know and own to competently pilot their investing ship are: *cash*, *bonds*, and *stocks*. In many situations, you can mentally add cash to bonds as the less volatile "conservative" or "income" side of your portfolio, while stocks constitute the "aggressive" or "growth" side of your portfolio. So, at its simplest, asset allocation can boil down to just two numbers: your stock allocation and your bond/cash allocation.

Drilling down within your stock holdings, there are three asset classes of interest: U.S. stocks, international stocks, and real estate or REIT (Real Estate Investment Trust) stocks. The majority of your stock holdings should typically be U.S. stocks, simply because the U.S. still has the most efficient and transparent financial system in the world, and U.S. corporations still comprise the majority of leading companies, globally. However, given long-term prospects for the U.S. economy, it is wise to have a substantial allocation to international stocks as well. Lastly, real estate is an important asset class that has historically generated wealth while being uncorrelated (moving inversely) to the stock market. So, if you don't already own investment real estate, such as a rental property, separately from your home, you should invest a portion of your equity (stock) assets into real estate, possibly REIT's.

As promised above, I'm going to show you here just one

example allocation, a conservative "all-weather" or "middle-ground" portfolio. This could be suitable for somebody approaching retirement, or for a younger investor who doesn't yet know his or her risk tolerance, or for a savvy older investor who needs some growth along with protection from market downturns.

Table: Asset Allocation for Generic "All-Weather" 50/50 Portfolio

Asset Type	% of Portfolio	% of Portfolio: Details
Income: cash/bonds	50%	40% bonds + 10% cash
Equities: stocks	50%	25% U.S. + 17.5% international + 7.5% real estate

Rebalancing

The most complex and hotly debated aspect of passive index investing, after the initial asset allocation, might be *rebalancing* – the periodic effort (often, but not necessarily, *annually*) to keep your portfolio asset classes close to their original allocation by selling winners and buying losers as values fluctuate over time.

Unfortunately, while there is a general consensus that rebalancing is a good thing, and numerous financial advisors are happy to do it for you and charge a fee, there is essentially *no* consensus on when or how to do it! Not only that, when you examine the research related to rebalancing, as I have done, it is difficult to find any consistent, compelling evidence proving it is more profitable over the long haul than simply leaving your portfolio alone!

Conclusion: You can likely forego explicit rebalancing for some time, until you've developed your own experience and opinions on the subject. What you *can* do to accomplish a similar objective, assuming you are saving consistently from your paycheck each month, is to direct that regular stream of savings into the assets that appear to be doing *worst*. You want to "buy low." So if the stock market is bubbly, you would buy bonds. If bond prices are high, you would buy stocks. And, if you aren't sure, you'd split the difference.

Learning More

Finally, there are hundreds of excellent books and web sites, including CanIRetireYet.com, on the subject of passive index investing. See the Resources page there for some suggestions.

And let me refer you to a select few resources right now:

- William Bernstein: *The Four Pillars of Investing: Lessons for Building a Winning Portfolio*

- Burton G. Malkiel: *The Random Walk Guide to Investing*

- Harry Browne: *Fail-Safe Investing: Lifelong Financial Security in 30 Minutes*

- Mike Piper: *Oblivious Investor*

Take Action

- Establish some emergency savings in a safe, insured bank account: 3-6 months of living expenses, enough to float you between jobs, if necessary. You can't sow the seeds for financial independence when you are living paycheck-to-paycheck. You need a buffer, some breathing room, in order to make good decisions. And you need the experience of saving and managing a small amount of money, before you aim higher.

- Begin investing early and keep it simple with passive index investing. Start small so you get a feel for how markets perform, before you must make major decisions. Invest steadily and learn essential behaviors while the stakes are low. By the time your investments grow large, and the market takes a tumble, you'll have the experience to handle it.

- If you don't have an account with one of the four customer-centric custodians listed before – Vanguard, USAA, Schwab, or Fidelity – or another that you trust completely, then go online to one of those web sites and open an account today.

- Choose a starting asset allocation. Buy small amounts each of a low-cost broad stock fund, and a low-cost broad bond fund, and begin to get the real-world experience of owning and monitoring your own investments.

■ Keep learning: Read everything you can on investing and personal finance. Develop your knowledge of the stock market and work towards understanding your own risk tolerance.

■ If you need confidence for making important investing decisions, an investing mentor could be the answer. Mine came in the form of a monthly investment newsletter. There are many such services available, though you'll have to do some research to find one that matches your philosophy.

■ If you need more guidance on a specific decision, consider an individual advisor, but make that choice very carefully, paying attention to costs. And, as soon as you're ready, take steps to wean yourself from any advisor.

■ When raises, bonuses, or good fortune come your way, enjoy a small splurge, then invest the balance. Don't make permanent changes to your lifestyle.

PART FOUR: ACCELERATING YOUR RETIREMENT

"The cost of a thing is the amount of what I will call life which is required to be exchanged for it, immediately or in the long run."
— Henry David Thoreau

"Frugality is important - to a point. But after we cut back to a reasonable level, our biggest win will come from earning more money." — Ramit Sethi

This book began with your financial dashboard – your spending, savings, and net worth. Next we explored the concept of "retirement," and *your* retirement in particular – your desired lifestyle and how much it will cost. Then we looked at the essential tools for achieving financial independence – the various savings vehicles, custodians, and managers for your money, plus passive index investing.

Now that we've laid the foundation, we come to the essence of this book: *accelerating* your retirement. First we'll examine what is possible: How soon could you actually retire? Then, to bring that goal even closer, I will explain the key money-saving strategies that I used on my own journey to early retirement. You'll learn all my best tips for spending less – from daily expenses to big-ticket items. Taken together, these techniques can bring your financial independence many years closer, while still letting you enjoy and savor life.

Finally, I'll explore the other side of the equation: how to increase your *income*, including the four proven strategies I've seen work in my life, and the lives of other successful early retirees, for building wealth. Whether you earn raises at work, generate profits from your own business, produce growth and income from your investments, or collect rents from your property portfolio – it all flows to your bottom line. And the wealth that you inevitably accumulate represents money, time, and – most importantly – *freedom,* to live the life you choose.

If you want to retire earlier than average, then you can't live an average life. You must spend much less, or make much more, and preferably both. The pages that follow will show you how....

17. Your Savings Rate: How Soon Can You Retire?

Before we look at the math, let's consider the big picture for early retirement. Simply put, to become financially independent, you must accumulate enough of the world's income-producing assets, that they can provide for your essential living needs indefinitely, without you having to work any longer.

How do you accomplish that? Well, you must *save*, and save a lot.

As always, there are two sides to saving. It helps to have substantial *income* to save from in the first place. And the surest way to get that high income in today's world is with an in-demand professional or technical education. Though there are other business and investing paths that we'll explore later in the book.

The second side to saving is controlling *expenses* – frugality. It helps if you have modest tastes and a penchant for managing money. The problem for most people is that they consume all of their assets as soon as they earn them. Some consume even more than that, going into debt.

How do you break that cycle of overconsumption? You must hitch up some creative frugality to a worthy goal like financial independence and motivate yourself to develop new habits. If you want to retire sooner, you can't live like everyone else.

When you put the two sides of saving together from a cash flow perspective, you wind up with your *savings rate* – the amount of your income, as a percent, that you are able to save instead of consuming. Interestingly, that single number captures all of the relevant factors for financial independence: how much you make, how much you consume, and how much is left over. And, it turns out, that it is the single most important factor in being able to retire early. *Nothing else comes close.* Amazingly, it doesn't even really matter how much you make: It's what's left over each month that counts over the long haul.

Let's look at the numbers. The following table which I've developed shows how many years it will take to retire at different savings rates:

Table: **How Many Years Will It Take?**

Savings Rate	Years to Retire
10%	38.3
15%	32.7
20%	28.6
25%	25.3
30%	22.6
35%	20.2
40%	18.1
45%	16.1
50%	14.3
55%	12.6
60%	11.1
65%	9.5
70%	8.1
75%	6.7
80%	5.3

(**Note**: The calculations behind this table assume that your consumption, what you don't save, stays relatively constant over your life. It also uses conventional values of an 8% portfolio return and a 4% safe withdrawal rate. Those numbers are historically accurate, but may be optimistic in today's world. The calculation also ignores taxes, inflation, and Social Security. So this is a greatly simplified, but still very useful, model for demonstrating the importance of savings rates. Just understand that it may not accurately predict *your* future: Your actual time to retirement could be more or less, depending on many factors.)

By studying the table above we can gain a better understanding of the forces at work in early retirement. Specifically, we can see the following important facts:

- Unless you can save more than 10% of your income, you will be stuck in the conventional 40-year or more working career, with retirement likely not possible until your 60's, or later.

- By saving 20% or so of your income over your career and investing it wisely, you can reasonably hope to retire around age 50. That was my route, and it worked.

- Though it won't be for everyone, by adopting an extremely frugal lifestyle, and saving half or more of your income, it is actually feasible to retire after less than a decade or two of work. (For real-world examples of people who have done this, see Mr. Money Mustache or Early Retirement Extreme.)

Perhaps the most important conclusion of all is this: *You can substantially accelerate your retirement by increasing your savings rate – making more and spending less.* Even for lower savings rates, the results are dramatic. Pump up your savings rate from 10% to 20% and you'll shave nearly 10 years off your working life! Increase it from 20% to 30% and you will add another 6 years to your early retirement.

Those numbers are feasible for many frugal, high-income workers: I know, because I did it.

Getting a marketable education and landing a good-paying job is a very helpful first step to financial independence. But what you do *next* makes all the difference. Will you inexorably step up your lifestyle and consume all that you bring in? Or will you save a significant percentage of your income to build wealth and reach financial independence sooner?

Living below your means, so that you create wealth with your free cash flow, is *key* to assembling riches and creating financial freedom for yourself. Saving 15% of your income is a common recommendation for retiring at age 65. But you'll want to aim much higher than that, saving at least 20-30% if possible, to build wealth and achieve financial freedom ahead of schedule.

18. Cutting Expenses: 12 Ways to Spend Less

Cutting expenses is a potent, double-edge sword for slaying the early retirement dragon. Why? Because not only does it produce more savings *now*, while you are working, but it also *reduces* the amount of savings that you need to accumulate for retirement, because your future living expenses will be lower too. As always, living below your means is key to accelerating your retirement.

Spending less is the simplest, most direct way to increase your effective income, and build wealth. Living cheaply is a strategy that you can apply every day, and it's *easy* once you get in the habit. Done right, being thrifty is fun and liberating. But it does require some energy and attention to detail. So it's important to stay motivated by keeping your end goal in mind: the freedom of financial independence.

Start by identifying and focusing on reductions in your top few expense categories. For most people, these will loom large: *housing, food, transportation, health care, recreation*. Brainstorm ways you can significantly reduce spending in these areas, and you will reap huge dividends in your progress toward financial independence.

To help you with specifics, the following are my favorite tips and techniques for reducing or controlling your expenses....

Pace Yourself

Learn not to spend impulsively. Set some personal expense

thresholds and keep them in mind. For purchases above those amounts, put them on a list, and study them first. Read reviews, ask questions, consider alternatives. Don't rush.

Use *wish lists*, such as those on amazon.com, to delay and defuse the need for instant gratification. I have extensive wish lists that I use to queue up books, music, and other things I *might* buy some day. Keeping them on a wish list ensures I won't forget about them. I even get some "ownership" pleasure from the things on my list, and some benefit from reading associated reviews. And I often find, as time goes on, that I don't really need things that looked appealing at first. In other cases, the right time comes, and I can take advantage of a special discount, or add one of those wish list items to another order, and save on shipping costs.

Try limiting major purchases to certain seasons, and deferring spending otherwise. For example, the end of the summer, and the New Year, can be natural times to evaluate and buy, if necessary. This saves you from having to think about major purchases during other periods in the year. And it may let you take advantage of sales and get better deals.

But allow yourself to splurge at certain times or in certain areas. Maybe it's a special day of the week, or after a hard workout, or anything under $5. Just be mindful whether your splurges are becoming obsessions that threaten your financial welfare: Are they happening more than once or twice a week? Are they constituting more than a percent or two of your monthly spending? Then, those are more than just splurges. Otherwise, don't fret about them.

Minimize Stuff

Most of us eventually learn that possessions don't create happiness. In fact, you may well discover that, as often as not, they add complexity to your life and can bring unhappiness!

Ask yourself: Do I receive genuine value or satisfaction from a product or service that is equal to the life energy I have to spend on it? Often the answer will be "no," especially if that expense doesn't align with your deepest life values and purposes.

Beware of complex or specialized devices whose purpose is to "save time." I've found that the overhead to regularly using most household labor-saving devices is usually much higher than expected. Once the novelty wears off, most tools and appliances gather dust in a corner somewhere. (As I write this, we have a large box on the porch of unused kitchen gadgets, headed to the next yard sale.)

Go slow when upgrading. More often than not, newer "improved" versions of things, just aren't. Sometimes they are more powerful, or easier to use. But much of the time they offer the same core functionality, along with more complexity, more fragility, cheaper parts, and new less-important features that detract from the main function. Moral: Defer buying the next generation until the current generation actually breaks.

Most modern tools and appliances have their own maintenance schedules: subsystems to be disassembled and cleaned, oil to be changed, filters to be replaced, and so on. Is your chore list full of tasks created by the *things* you've accumulated? When something you own creates more work than it saves, get rid of it!

Cut Recurring Expenses

Whether your goal is building wealth, retiring early, or just making your dollars go farther, cutting *recurring expenses* will pay huge dividends. Here I'm talking about regular – usually monthly – charges such as phone bills, gym memberships, or property insurance. These are important, and insidious, for several reasons:

1. They are often fully automated expenses, so they will never end, unless you take action.

2. Companies are adept at making them easy to add on impulse (requiring a simple consent or web form), but hard to cancel (requiring a phone call or sometimes written communication).

3. They often appear small, but in fact can be very substantial, especially from a retirement perspective...

Why are recurring expenses of particular concern when thinking about retirement? Because of what I will call the **Rule of 300**. It goes like this: *The amount of money you must save to meet a monthly expense in retirement is approximately 300 times that expense.*

That's right! So if you commit to a seemingly insignificant $30/month membership that you plan to keep indefinitely, you need to save $30 x 300 = $9,000 to pay for that membership, once you stop working!

Where does that 300 factor come from? It's derived from the 4% safe withdrawal rate we discussed earlier. Remember that the inverse of 4% (1 divided by 0.04) gives a multiplier of 25x. And, of course to convert a monthly expense to an annual one, you must multiple by 12 months, so that's our second multiplier. Next, combine the multipliers, 25 x 12 and you get the **Rule of 300** multiplier for the amount you must save to provide for a certain monthly expense in retirement.

So recurring expenses – even small ones – deserve serious consideration and analysis, before signing on the bottom line. Now, I'm a big fan of occasional *splurges* – treats that help keep life fun on the long road to financial independence. But I set a very high bar for committing to any *recurring* expenses, and recommend you do the same. Before you decide any kind of ongoing commitment is "cheap," multiply it by 300 and then picture how long it will take you to save that sum!

Now that you know how important it is to control your recurring expenses, here is a list you can review to jog your memory. Can you cut in any of these areas?

- memberships
- maintenance
- subscriptions
- insurance
- telephone

- services

- rentals

- fees

- utilities

Remember, companies have little incentive to go out of their way to help you minimize your bills. Their policies and procedures are necessarily oriented to persuading you to tack additional charges onto your monthly bill. Believe it or not, a mere "dollar a day" expense actually represents about $9,000 in required savings for retirement!

Optimize Housing

Your home is one of life's largest expenses, and perhaps the one most subject to vanity. Before moving or upgrading, ask whether you can stay in your existing home instead. And, if it's more than you need, downsize to a smaller home or condo as soon as practical. Unused or unneeded space is an ongoing waste of your financial resources.

In general, pay off your mortgage as soon as possible. When investment yields are low, and returns unpredictable, using extra income to pay down a high-rate mortgage loan can be an excellent investment. In some cases it may make sense to keep paying a low-rate mortgage. But don't underestimate the peace of mind and confidence that come from living totally debt free.

Be very careful about home improvement projects. It's

possible to spend vast sums of money on your home without measurably improving your quality of life. And, as mentioned earlier, the old rules about getting that money back when you sell have changed: The return on a remodeling investment has eroded substantially in the last decade. If your home is already safe and comfortable, don't borrow to improve it, even against its own equity.

In fact, don't spend on anything that doesn't give you an immediate benefit. Trying to create the perfect home is a never-ending battle. Construction materials, home furnishings, and appliances are imperfect and wear out. We've seen expensive carpets get trashed by teenagers, nice furniture get shredded by pets, high-end stainless steel appliances get scratched and discolored, and beautiful granite countertops trash an entire wardrobe: a rough spot at the sink wore holes in all of our clothes!

Fine-Tune Your Food

Food is the most frequent major expense, and it is intimately tied up with health. Awareness pays dividends here too. Cook at home more. Simplify meals. Store and use leftovers. Eat lower on the food chain, if you can.

A simple technique that will also save you time and gas is to shop just once a week. Buy in bulk, and buy on sale. Then don't buy food between shopping trips. Make do with what you have until the next weekly trip. Find recipes online for what you have on hand. Monitor your pantry and fridge to prevent spoilage and waste: See what's nearing expiration and eat it before it goes bad.

Is there an expensive prepared food that you just love? Develop your own recipe. It will be cheaper, and probably healthier for you. We've done that for energy bars and tea drinks with great success.

If you find you are spending a lot on groceries, break it down. Analyze a few grocery bills and find out where the money is going. Then prune. In our case we realized we were spending too much on expensive juice drinks, and were letting fresh produce go to waste. By concentrating on those, and other areas, we were able to reduce our grocery bill by about 20%!

Dining Out

One of the budget categories we've had to watch carefully over the years is *dining out*. That is, and always has been, one of our "luxuries." Many years ago, we adopted a simple and painless mechanism to enforce that part of the budget. Each month we deposit our budgeted amount into a small *change purse* as cash. (If you want to forego cash, you could use one or more debit cards to control spending on certain budget categories.) That purse holds our strict allotment for dining out each month. We can spend it on a few elegant evenings, or on a number of take-out dinners plus some coffee shop treats. The choice is ours. But when the cash runs out each month, we stop dining out until the next month's resupply.

That purse gives us a simple visual reminder of how much we have left in the dining out category each month. In fact, it encourages us to spend joyfully. It's "mad money" that we've purposefully set aside, and we never feel any guilt or stress around spending it. And, a side benefit of paying for most of our dining out in cash is that we have fewer receipts to manage. There is no need to track just where or when we've spent that money, so long as we know the monthly total that is going to eating out. Thus, we cut down on paperwork.

Tune Up Transportation

It's financially and emotionally liberating to disengage your self-image from the vehicle you drive. Yes, we *did* own Swedish imports during the peak of our career and child-rearing years, but have been downshifting and downsizing ever since. As this is written, we own a 6-year-old Toyota and a 7-year-old Ford-based camper van.

Drive modest vehicles, purchased *used* if possible, instead of the latest hot models. Smaller vehicles cost less up front, consume less gas, are easier to drive and park, and can still earn high safety ratings. And buying used means you miss the punishing first year of depreciation.

Maintain vehicles well: Do it yourself when possible or use a local mechanic instead of the dealer. And drive those vehicles longer. Most modern vehicles can give reliable service well after turning 100,000 miles, if properly cared for. When something major goes wrong, carefully evaluate the repair/replacement decision. It often makes economic sense to do major repairs, even on older vehicles, especially if you can get a warranty on the work.

Downsize your vehicle *count* too. Do without that extra vehicle. You can share a car, car pool, use public transportation, or even bike, walk or scooter to your destinations. When I retired, I gave up having my own around-town car, and now share the smaller car with Caroline. I expected that to be hard, emotionally and practically. It wasn't. It's no big deal to coordinate my trips with hers. And it's great having one less vehicle to maintain and insure.

Enjoy Cheap Vacation Travel

Vacations and travel are an essential part of what makes life worth living for many of us. Nearly all of my cherished family memories come from our travels. I wouldn't trade those memories for anything, and I'm so grateful that our generally frugal lifestyle never precluded seeing and experiencing the world in new and exciting ways.

But we did it on a budget. It's critical not to let expensive travel become the safety valve for a stressful lifestyle or a job that no longer suits you. It's pointless to work a high-stress, high-paying job with long hours just so you can blow many thousands of dollars every year on exotic vacations in an attempt to undo the damage. Even if you must work that kind of job for a period of time, cultivate the ability to decompress closer to home, and less expensively. That will keep you on the road to financial freedom.

The majority of our family vacations involved *driving* and *camping*. I personally prefer to avoid air travel whenever possible. It's necessary at times, and isn't necessarily expensive, depending on when you buy tickets. But a huge drawback is that it leaves you without a bed, meals, and transportation on the other end of the flight. Providing those – hotels, restaurants, and rental cars – for more than a few days, can ratchet up travel costs quickly. A camper van provides an ideal solution for our vacation travel. It's a bit more expensive to drive, but generally pays that back in reduced lodging, food, and transportation costs, as long as we are staying for a while on the other end.

Of course, camping may not be for you, or you may not have a relaxed vacation schedule that can accommodate driving. There are still numerous creative solutions for cheap travel. From sites that allow you to bid on airfares and lodging (Google for "travel price comparison"), to sites that facilitate house swapping (Google for "home exchange"), to sites that feature do-it-yourself rentals (Google for "owner vacation rentals"), the web is a gold mine of possibilities for cheaper travel. *One final key point*: Always plan your adventures far enough in advance that you can optimize and take advantage of the best deals.

Focus on Health

Health insurance and health care may the toughest of all costs to control. In today's world, individuals have very little leverage versus the health care establishment.

But you can start by taking good care of yourself first, through diet and exercise. Your health is both a quality of life *and* a financial issue. The potential cost savings of a healthy lifestyle, especially in your later years, are enormous. If you can't get motivated in other ways, think of all the money you'll save by being healthy! Physical and mental health are the foundation for enjoying the rest of life: other goals, including financial goals, don't make much sense without it.

Eat moderately, eat well, and exercise regularly. A simple route to better health for all of us, including the planet, is to cultivate *free, green fun*. In keeping with cutting recurring expenses, avoid activities with ongoing fees. Anything that involves self-propelled activity on public lands, or in public facilities, is an excellent choice. Find what works for you.

Start by walking, hiking, or running. Move on to swimming or road biking. Throw in some team sports if that's your thing. Or advance to paddling, climbing, or mountain biking, if you're able and willing. Some of these activities require modest expenses up front, but then cost very little for a lifetime of enjoyment. They'll keep you in good health, minimize impact on the planet, and are fun and exciting. What's not to like?

Self-Insure When Possible

Some people have an affinity for insurance and buy all the coverage they can get. It gives them peace of mind, for a price. Others are suspicious of insurance and loathe paying premiums for services they may never use.

Count me in that latter camp. But, I've tried to be rational in evaluating insurance options. For example, there was never any question of carrying life insurance while our son was growing up. But as soon as he, and we, had clearly reached financial independence, I cancelled my large life insurance policy. There was no point in paying those hefty premiums, once we were no longer dependent on my income from work. Same story with disability insurance. (Though I have kept some inexpensive accidental disability coverage.)

The insurance industry has perfected its guilt pitch for life insurance: You are an irresponsible parent if you don't have insurance in place to care for your children if you were gone. *Probably true.* Yet the industry has extended that guilt trip willy-nilly. You're being reckless or thoughtless if you don't buy every new insurance product it invents.

Some insurance is clearly redundant. Why would you need payment protection insurance on your consumer debt, for example, if you have decent life and disability coverage and a reasonable debt level? Adequate life and disability insurance are meant to cover all your financial obligations, including bills, if you are gone or incapacitated.

And beware that insurance doesn't just make covered problems disappear. You still have paperwork, deductibles, copays, coinsurance, and time limits to contend with. And that assumes the insurance company accepts your claims. Most insurance is better understood as a way to *defray* costs.

I believe in **self-insuring** *whenever you can.* Remember that insurance is generally a kind of *business*, run at a profit. That means that whenever you can reasonably self-insure, you will *also* turn a profit. You'll come out ahead in the long run.

But before you cancel or reduce coverage, and put

yourself or loved ones at risk, you must ask yourself some tough questions:

1.   Will you be "in business" to pay a claim? This is why you can't self-insure for life (or disability) insurance, at least not as long as you have dependents relying on you for income. If they need you to be alive and working to put bread on the table, then part of caring for them is buying enough insurance so they are not destitute should you pass away. But there is still room for discretion in determining *how much* life insurance you should buy. The insurance industry has rules of thumb for why you should buy a lot. I think that's a personal decision and depends in part on where your dependents are in life. If they are healthy, my opinion is that you should buy enough insurance to give them a generous cushion for transitioning their lives (or growing up), but not necessarily so much that they become independently wealthy by virtue of your departure.

2.   Could you afford to pay a claim from your *liquid assets*? It's not enough just to be "in business." You've got to have the cash to make good on a loss, without taking losses elsewhere. That's why people shouldn't self-insure their homes or health care – because the potential costs and consequences are so high. Very few people keep six-digit sums of cash lying around – and those are the potential losses when it comes to your home or health. However you *can*

crank up those deductibles, to reduce your premiums.

You might be able to self-insure your auto in some cases. Auto liability coverage is required by law in most states, so that's not an option, but dropping auto collision coverage can be viable. To do that, you must keep $5,000-$10,000, or whatever you think you'd need to pick up some functional used transportation on short notice, available in a savings account or low-volatility investment. And I'll guess that's where most people get cold feet and decide to pay an insurance premium instead: It would be a lot of cash to part with all at once. Just be advised, you're effectively making the same payment, over time, via an insurance premium.

3. How *likely* is a claim? Insurance companies have the business volume and data to answer this question very precisely, and that's why they can run highly profitable businesses under conditions where we, as individuals, cannot. Still, there are situations where we have pretty good data, possibly even an edge over the insurance company. You know your family health history. You know the individuals in your family and how they behave. For example, after my son had been driving a few years, I dropped the collision coverage on his 12-year old vehicle. I knew he was an excellent driver, and a quick back-of-the envelope calculation told me that it just wasn't

worth the premium we were paying to insure the current salvage value of that vehicle, given the low probability of an accident. We could self-insure.

How does that math work? Well, here is a simple formula I learned for evaluating probabilistic problems in engineering school: **loss * probability = premium**. So if you're putting a vehicle worth $5,000 at 5% risk of loss annually, a "break-even" premium would be about $250/year. Anything higher than that, and you're better off self-insuring. (An actuary could provide a more sophisticated analysis, but I suspect this is close enough for many purposes.)

Self insuring can be *scary*, no doubt. Sometimes insurance feels cheap for the peace of mind conferred. For example, I've made some impulse insurance buys over the years related to major appliances. I generally abhor maintenance contracts and service plans, but, on a couple of occasions, when the appliance seemed expensive and the plan seemed cheap, I've gone for the bait. It's always been a mistake. We've yet to collect: all our appliances have outlived their service contracts without major repairs.

Similarly, I was once offered a service contract on our camper van for around $60/month that covered a litany of major problems for every system on our rig. The glossy brochure was complete with stories from grateful travelers who had major repair bills paid, and their vacations saved from heartbreak. I nearly took the bait again. But then I looked at the hefty deductible, and the low probability of most of the failures, and realized I'd make a profit if I self-insured. After a year had passed with no major problems, I'd already saved enough by *not* buying that policy to pay for the first major repair, if and when it should materialize.

I'll admit there is one area where I've always found it easy to justify a service contract: *my computers*. Access to a functioning computer has been critical to my livelihood ever since the start of my career. Being down, even for a few hours, is guaranteed to produce frustration, and possibly even loss of income. I've never had a problem paying a few hundred dollars a year to avoid that. Since computers were my profession, I had a good feel for the costs and benefits. And I've exercised those computer service contracts a number of times over the years.

Insuring my computers is essentially a business decision. Ideally, you should evaluate *all* insurance unemotionally, with the same hard look at the financial facts you'd use for running a business. Neutralize the sales pitch. Evaluate the probabilities versus the costs. And make a rational choice....

Avoid Changing Locations or Partners

Major life changes are inevitable, but they are often costly. To retire early and well – in some cases even to retire at all – it is critical to avoid the financial equivalent of a major detour or train wreck.

I'm talking here about expenses in the tens of thousands of dollars that can completely derail your savings plan. For most earners, that kind of money will take years to recover and will inevitably impact your confidence and determination to become financially independent.

That's a scenario to be avoided at all costs. Fortunately, two of the largest potential life expenses are avoidable for many.

Changing Homes

Let's start with a common, large change: moving between houses.

I grew up in a military family and was accustomed to moving every few years. I kept that wanderlust into my 20's. I had few possessions, and rented, so the trouble and expense of moving were manageable. Then I married, and we bought our first house, and had a child. Our next move was punishing. Because of market conditions in our town, we were forced to sell our house at a steep loss, and, because of all our new stuff, we had to hire professional movers for the first time. (My employer generously defrayed our expenses.) We moved two more times over the next few years, between rentals, then we bought another house and *stayed put* for more than 16 years. In retrospect, that final, settled destination was an *enormous* help in growing our assets and retiring early.

Based on our early moving experiences, I keep a ballpark cost figure in mind of $20,000 as a disincentive to relocating. Sound outrageous? According to an article in *SmartMoney*, the rule of thumb for closing costs to a home buyer is from 3% to 5% of the purchase price. For a relatively modest $200,000 home, that could mean as much as $10,000. The seller doesn't have mortgage-related costs, but is likely paying a realtor commission as high as 6%. Then there are moving costs. According to CostHelper.com, packing and relocating a 1,500 square-foot house across the country can set you back from $9,000 to $11,600. Even if you have less stuff, move closer, or do some of the work yourself, the cost will likely be in the thousands. Then there are the inevitable shakedown costs with any new home: new carpets and curtains, fresh paint, miscellaneous repairs, supplies and furnishings, and modifications to suit your lifestyle.

So, by the time you add up the costs of selling one home, relocating, buying another home, and settling into it, that $20,000 figure might be conservative! In short, changing homes is frightfully expensive, and will probably eat up most of the average family's potential savings for several years running.

Granted, there are unavoidable life scenarios, mostly job-related, where you don't have the luxury of choosing to stay put. But anytime the choice to move is yours, stop and consider the expenses. The worst choice possible is to move into a *bigger* house *nearby* that you don't really need. You are opting in to a large one-time expense, plus a bigger ongoing mortgage and maintenance obligation. If more space is truly necessary, consider instead *adding onto your current home*. (When our son reached the later teen years, we renovated a larger downstairs room so he could have more space.)

If you must relocate for work, consider renting for a while in the new location so you have the experience and information to make the best possible decision before buying a new house. If you are voluntarily choosing to relocate to another area of the country for lifestyle reasons, then take the time to make the optimal decision. We spent a year making our last relocation decision: did weeks of research, travelled to our candidate locations multiple times, then rented in the new area for 6 months before buying the home where we have now lived happily for many years.

Changing Marriages

The second major life change is one we should have the most control over – changing partners.

By some estimates, nearly half of marriages now end in divorce. Extrapolating from statistics in a recent report from the U.S. Department of Health and Human Services, divorces in the U.S. average somewhat over 1 *million* annually. Not only is breaking up with your partner stressful and tumultuous, but it is also extremely *expensive.* According to Forbes.com, the average cost of a divorce in the U.S. ranges from about $15,000 up to $30,000. Most of that goes to the lawyers and the courts. Divorce litigation is an astounding $28 billion/year industry!

The most important financial factor in divorce, though not technically an "expense," is even more devastating. In most divorce settlements your *net worth* will be cut in half, or worse, as you split assets with your former spouse (and the lawyers). If one person could live as cheaply as two, that wouldn't be so devastating. But, unfortunately, that's not the case: Sharing a home, vehicle, and meals are just three areas where quality of life is higher, and cheaper, with two people, than it is with one. So, aside from the immediate high legal expenses, the impact on your net worth of going through divorce is likely to set any retirement plans back years, or decades. To further compound the financial pain, divorce will often result in the sale of a home, plus two relocations. And, when alimony is involved, the financial costs continue into the future....

My focus here is personal finance. I'm not going to delve into what makes a strong marriage, except to observe how valuable one is from a financial perspective. And note the feedback loop at work in relationships: Mutual prudence and financial responsibility contribute to a strong marriage, and a strong marriage contributes to stronger finances in the long run. So working to stabilize and strengthen your relationship will pay off not only in more peace and joy in your everyday life, but in a healthy financial bottom line as well.

Unfortunately, not all relationships will last. But appreciating the financial consequences might add some motivation to make good decisions up front, invest in the relationship you already have, and avoid a major financial catastrophe. Creating a stable long-term relationship will contribute mightily to both your happiness, and financial well-being.

Choose Your "Luxuries"

It's safe to say that most of us in line to become financially independent or retire early do not lead lives of luxury. For example, I shave with bar soap, buy socks at Walmart, don't pay for cable, and didn't own a smartphone for years.

Frugality is a necessary baseline for most who build wealth. But does this mean that luxuries are bad? And what exactly is a "luxury" anyway? Could it be different for different people?

The dictionary tells us that a luxury is "something inessential, but conducive to pleasure and comfort." But that definition leaves quite a bit of room for interpretation.

To be *essential* is to be close to the essence of something, inherent, almost a part of it.

What is truly essential to human life? Water, food, clothing, shelter, companionship.... It's a short list. And, at least in the developed world, easily or freely obtained by most of us. Does that mean that everything else – from bicycles to BMWs, from ginger spice to ice cream, from watches to iPhones – is a luxury?

When it comes to evaluating an expense for the kind of frugal living that leads to financial independence, I think it's more useful to focus on the following three factors, rather than on whether something is a "luxury" or not by somebody else's standards:

1. What are its features, in addition to its core function?

2. What is its value to you, in relation to its cost?

3. What is its overall cost, in relation to your living expenses?

Take *cars*, for example. The core function of a vehicle

is to transport you, and some of your stuff, from one place to another. Onboard navigation systems, iPod integration, rearview cameras, and 400 horsepower with paddle shifters really are supplementary to that goal! However, corporate marketing machines have been very effective at creating "artificial" functions for your vehicle, such as enhancing your self-image, or rewarding you for having "arrived."

When we bought our Toyota Prius in 2007, we wound up with the Touring model because it was already on the lot, in the color we wanted, and the dealer was willing to negotiate aggressively on price. What made it a "Touring" model? Alloy wheels with slightly larger (and harder to find and more expensive) tires, and a slightly larger rear spoiler. *Utter foolishness*, since discontinued by Toyota. I'm glad we didn't pay more for these "luxuries," which turned out to be liabilities, in this case. But we do love our Prius – primarily because it has been cheap, functional, trouble-free transportation.

Or take our 2006 camper van. If purchased new (we got ours *used*), it would cost as much as a BMW 7 Series sedan. Is our camper van a luxury vehicle then? It's a lot slower, noisier, and harder to drive than a BMW sedan. We're somewhat less comfortable in it than we are in our full-size house or even a hotel room. On the other hand it's a *lot* more comfortable than camping in a tent or pop-up trailer. And, by letting us cut lodging costs and prepare our own food on the road, it enables a mobile lifestyle and long, inexpensive vacations that have been steadily earning back the initial cost.

Luxuries are fun. They make life more pleasurable and

comfortable. In a world of infinite resources, most of us would add all the luxuries we could on top of life's necessities. But, alas, we only have so much money, and so much time, to buy, learn, maintain, and play with our stuff. So, before each purchase, we need to decide: *Is this truly valuable to me?*

And, how do you know that? Ask yourself a few questions: How many hours do I have to work to afford this? How many hours will I use it? Will I still benefit from it a year from now? Is there a better way to spend my money?

The primary luxury in my life for many years was my mountain bike. I rode a near-competition-level bike from a small, trendy U.S. bike manufacturer, outfitted with top-of-the line components. Though I got a deal on it from a friend in the business, it retailed for what would be a generous month's pay for many. Outrageous to spend that much on a bicycle, right? Yet I never regretted this luxury in my life. I could easily afford it (in part because we own so few other luxuries) and it gave me riding confidence on countless great backcountry adventures with my son. When it was stolen, I was content to replace it with a recreational-level bike at less than one-third the cost, because I no longer valued the luxury in that area of my life.

That brings us to a final question for evaluating luxuries in your life: *Can you afford it?* The issue with luxuries isn't that they are inherently evil or inappropriate. The problem is when you develop habits to the point that expensive luxuries become necessities that you want all the time, or in every area of your life.

Take the well-worn "latte factor." It's hard to find a personal finance web site without either an article or calculator showing you how much you could save toward retirement if you swore off expensive coffee drinks.

Well, I have a confession. We like coffee shops and bakeries. Sometimes (usually on vacation), we go to them. But we've never lived near one, so it's never been part of our daily routine. It's just a fun splurge. And it's never enough money to be more than a blip on our monthly spending. We could probably even afford a latte a day if we wanted, but then that would start to crowd out other potential luxuries. And coffee just isn't that important to us.

So, when thinking about the expenses in your life, ask yourself these three questions:

1. *Is this optional?* If so, then it is, to some extent, a *luxury* – and you should give it a little more thought before proceeding.

2. *Is this truly important to me?* If it's something you value, over almost anything else, then you should prioritize that expense. As long as you can answer this third question:

3. *Can I afford it?* Is it less than a few percent of your monthly budget, or does it enable long-term, quantifiable savings or quality of life? If so, go for it. Otherwise, don't go there….

Leverage Generosity

Set an annual budget for your charitable contributions. Then keep track of your individual contributions during the year, to ensure you are prioritizing the organizations you value most. It's also helpful to keep track of what you gave in previous years, for comparison.

Charities, like other direct mail operations, pelt you with numerous solicitations throughout the year. If you don't keep track of your giving, you may find that your donations over time don't match your priorities. I keep a checklist of my currently designated charities next to our junk mail recycling bin. If I get a solicitation from an organization not on the list, or one on the list that I've already donated to for the year, it goes into recycling, unopened.

There seems to be a higher law of money: *Generosity leads to wealth.* I know that one of the happiest and most prosperous years of my life was also one when I was most generous. And I'm not sure which was the cause and which the effect. They seem to be interrelated. Generously and wisely allocating resources without desperately hanging on to each dollar is a mindset that also leads to recognizing and capitalizing on opportunities for personal prosperity. *And it just feels good.*

19. Boosting Income:
4 Ways to Get Rich Quicker

What's the surest path to riches?

Since the dawn of history, people have fretted over this question, throwing themselves into schemes and enterprises to create wealth. Usually those schemes have promised to produce money quicker and with less effort than ever before. More often than not, they haven't delivered....

Whether it's been trading tulip bulbs, sailing to the New World, traveling west to stake a claim, trading Internet stocks, or flipping real estate, the results have often been the same. A few lucky souls – usually the early arrivals – have done well. Some others – by taking on substantial risk and adding large amounts of sweat equity – have done OK. And many more – the late arrivals, the unmotivated, the underachievers – have lost more than they gained.

I know a little about building wealth, having reached financial independence and retired early. But I don't know how to "get rich quick." I guess it's possible. A few people seem to have done it. But the process likely involves personal or situational elements, and a dash of luck, that can't be easily duplicated. The only "quick" wealth I've seen has come from a foundation that was long in the making.

Preparation, *patience*, and *persistence* are common themes in all the wealth building I've personally witnessed, and those qualities are foundational to the wealth-building paths I'm about to discuss....

It Begins with You...

Much as we might wish otherwise, the capacity for wealth starts within ourselves, yes, within *you*. Sure, some of us will inherit money, or connections, or game-changing talents. And most of us will be the beneficiaries of some generosity – perhaps financial, but more likely advice, support, and opportunity – along the way.

But nobody else, no external force, can bestow on you the potential to create wealth. That potential is a natural outcome of your capacity to create value for other human beings. And where does that capacity come from? In today's world, primarily from your *skills*, and what you make of them. So the starting point for building wealth has to be equipping yourself with a skill set that leverages your talents to create value for others, generally by getting and continuing an *education* that is valued in the marketplace.

That doesn't always have to be a formal education – it could come from the real world. I learned everything I know about software engineering *after* graduating from college. Some individuals are born with innate business or investing skills, and the drive and opportunity to take advantage of them. But, regardless of where you start, you must keep learning and developing skills throughout your career, if you want to maximize your earning potential. I would never have landed in a profitable business if I had stopped learning after college. And most of the skills I needed at the end of my successful career were completely different from those I depended on early and mid-career.

Once you are in a career that creates value in the world, you will have access to the initial income stream that can help you build wealth. So now that you have that cash flow, what do you do with it?

Well, there are three additional paths that I know from experience you can travel to create more wealth in your life. I've leveraged two of them myself: investing in the stock market and starting a business, while I've seen many others profit from the third path: rental real estate.

Investing in the Stock Market

Earlier, we discussed how buying stocks and bonds is an essential tool for achieving financial independence. It is probably the most accessible path to wealth. And, I explained how *passive index investing* is the surest route to investing success for most people. However, as a rule, that investing strategy is neither especially quick nor overly profitable, because its goal is to *match* market returns.

As long as you are around investing, you'll continue to hear the siren song of outperforming the market. You can't read financial news without being pelted with strategies, funds, and advisors who have *recently* outperformed the market, and are now inviting you to do the same. It is ever-so-tempting to think you can retire sooner through somehow gaming the stock market by actively trading. But be advised that very few succeed.

A time-tested principle of investing is that the only way

to elevate profits is to take on more risk. And that has its own downside. Taking on extra investing risk in today's world generally means dealing in more complex or specialized niches. And I don't generally recommend that. You'd be playing in a game of full-time professionals, one that is stacked against you.

So are there any safe routes you can take to enhance your investments, or outperform passive index investing?

There is one investing technique that I believe allows for taking on more risk in a structured and predictable manner, that can pay off if you are a studious and disciplined investor. This is *dividend* or *value stock picking*. It's an investment philosophy established by Benjamin Graham and others, and popularized in our era by Warren Buffett. It involves buying stocks whose prices appear to be undervalued through an analysis of fundamentals like financial statements, management, competition, and markets. The essence of value investing is buying stocks "on sale," at less than some expected intrinsic value, which will provide you with a margin of safety. (For example: If you got a great deal on a used car, you'd have money left over to spend on repairs, if that turns out to be necessary. But it may not be.)

Influential studies have shown that value stocks outperform growth stocks over the long term by a couple of percentage points or more. These stocks also have the beneficial property of paying higher regular dividends. So you get a steady stream of income while you wait for a payback on the initial investment. The downsides of value investing are that it requires more skill and time to implement, and there is danger of taking on risk due to lack of diversification. There are plenty of value mutual funds and ETFs available, but it is difficult to maximize your income without picking *individual* stocks. And those tend to be concentrated in potentially volatile industries like banking and energy. Another concern is that you must have the discipline to hang on to your value stocks for the very long term, to see all the expected rewards.

In summary, value stock investing is a proven long-term investment strategy, one that has historically outperformed broad-based passive index investing. But it typically requires more skill and patience on the investor's part. And there is no guarantee that history will repeat. For those reasons, I'll continue to advise passive index investing for most of us, and leave further exploration of value stock picking as an exercise for interested readers. (If you are one of them, then you could do worse than to start with writings by and about Graham, Buffett, and my own investing mentor: Richard C. Young.)

Starting a Business

Starting and owning a business is probably the quickest path to wealth for many. Why? Because owning a business eliminates the middlemen between you and profits, allows you to leverage other people's time and money, and gives you valuable tax deductions and credits.

But starting a business is by no means the easiest, or the surest, route to wealth. It's usually back-breaking work, and also quite risky. A high percentage of business startups fail: According to the U.S. Small Business Administration, less than 50% of small businesses will survive their first five years! But if you are creative, with a strong work ethic, and have more time than money, then starting a business may be a good fit for you.

Business ownership was the beginning of my own path to wealth. A few years out of college, I went out on my own, first as a freelance technical writer and software consultant. Later, in the days before the Internet, I started a small software company selling hypertext references. That company did very well for a few years but, more importantly, it set me up for a merger with a larger company, where the real profits were.

Overall, I started or participated in 5 different small businesses over my 29-year career in software engineering. I made some mistakes but, ultimately, I was successful: I became financially independent and retired early.

What I'm going to do next is share with you my 7 essential business startup lessons learned, so you can fast-track your own success. This advice is a potential gold mine. The distilled wisdom from much of my working life, it has the potential to keep you out of dead ends and on the track to profits, if you take it to heart:

1. **Make sure there's a market**. Do everything possible at the start of your business to ensure there is a market for what you are selling, whether it be information, services, or widgets. This is why existing *competition* is generally a good thing. It assures you that customers exist. If your concept is totally new, or substantially

different from the competition, then conduct some quick, cheap tests to prove your idea has appeal. One of the best ways to start is to freelance on the side, or offer a small, streamlined, or prototype version for cheap or free. Sites like eBay, Craigslist, Elance, and Fiverr make this easy. Keep testing different ideas until you find the one that people will spend a few dollars on, or at least trade for their email address.

2.   **Focus on customers, not technology**. It's fun and exciting to learn the latest tools, and be a part of the latest technology buzz. But that's a backwards way to build a business. (Unless your business involves selling to other technologists!) Your customers don't care much about technology. They have real-world problems to solve and want practical solutions. Whether those solutions are built with the latest bleeding edge, or aging legacy technology, is largely unimportant to them, as long as it works and the price is right! At the beginning, only your customers and their problems matter.

3.   **Avoid infrastructure and build the core of your business**. The most critical question is this: *Can I deliver something compelling to customers willing to pay more for it than it costs me?* Do whatever it takes to answer that question as quickly as you can, and you will uncover a viable business. Avoid at all costs any overhead or infrastructure that gets in the way of answering that question. And, yes, I mean you should

skip, at the start, everything from writing a formal business plan, to incorporating, to printing business cards, to buying office equipment, setting up bank accounts, designing logos, and joining professional organizations. All that stuff that business "experts" say you need. Most of it, in most situations, will simply cost you time and money without bringing you any closer to the goal of getting customers and producing a profit!

4. **Be realistic about your skills.** Starting a business is hard. Many fail. Before jumping into a new venture, and especially before quitting your day job, ask yourself what gives you an edge? Why will you succeed? Focus on two areas: (1) your business domain skills, and (2) your networking and marketing skills. Do you know an in-demand business product or service so well that you can produce it very competitively with just a fraction of your available time – say 25%? Good, because you'll need to do that. You won't have the luxury of spending most of your time actually producing the product or service. Instead you'll be running and marketing your business. Next ask yourself, what gives you an edge in marketing? How will you get the word out, cheaply, so enough people take notice? Do you have a track record of doing this well, or can you partner with somebody who has? This is essential if paying customers are to find out about your business.

5. **Know when to do it yourself, and when to get help.**
This is the next step after realistically assessing your business idea, and yourself. Ask, "What is lacking?" Strongly prefer businesses where you already have all the necessary skills for the initial launch. Because then you can do everything that's required, cheaply, and on time. But, if you don't have all the skills, network with friends and colleagues to complement your skill set. Barter for tasks if possible. If necessary, pay for small freelance tasks through sources like 99designs, Elance, or Fiverr. Partner or hire employees only as a last resort – because then you are starting to add infrastructure before you even know if you have a viable business. It's much better to commit to such lasting relationships only as part of scaling out an already proven idea.

6. **Do something so good that it can't be ignored.**
The last time you encountered a mediocre, boring, or overpriced new product or service, did you buy it? *Exactly.* Don't expect to get sales, or even much interest, without that 'wow' factor. At least one dimension – quality, novelty, or price – and preferably more than one – should *impress* your customers. Otherwise they just won't notice you in today's sea of competing ideas. How do you get that 'wow' factor? Sometimes new technology, or stunning presentation, or breakthrough pricing can deliver the knockout punch. But behind those elements is always a more

traditional factor: hard work. That's right, at least at the start, you've got to *sweat the details*, go the extra mile, and pour additional value into your offering – so your customers don't have to.

7. **Diversify your revenue sources.** Ok, so you've followed all the steps up to this point. Do you have a viable business yet? Possibly. One last element to consider, before you take it to the bank, is this: How diverse is your customer base? Are you a consultant with just a couple customers? A retail operation with seasonal traffic? A software company with a single product? A web site that appeals only to frugal students? Even if it looks like a business, even if it is currently making a profit, it may not be viable in the long run. Some lost customers, a shift in fashion or demographics, could snuff you out. Don't rest until you have a diverse revenue stream – only then do you have a truly viable business.

Buying and Managing Rental Real Estate

We've already discussed the role of real property in your wealth – how home equity is a major savings vehicle for many, and how real estate can be an important diversifier in your investment portfolio.

Real estate is a proven investment that keeps up with inflation and can generally be safely financed with leverage – borrowed money. In fact, real estate is probably the oldest and most accessible path to wealth. Since recorded time, all kinds of people have owned property and rented out rooms, apartments, or houses. If you have some seed money – for a down payment, and some time – for maintenance and management, rental real estate could work for you, *accelerating* your savings.

If starting a new kind of business, or investing in stocks, strikes you as too complex or abstract, then *landlording* may be your path. People from all walks of life have been successful landlords. Buying and operating a portfolio of rental properties is a common and proven route to wealth for those with the right skill set and personality to maintain property and manage tenants.

But there is a cost: Rental real estate is as much a *business* as it is an *investment*. Property, and people, require maintenance. Property needs repairs and replacements, and taxes and insurance must be paid. People require contracts, and meetings, and reminders. You can do property maintenance and management yourself if you have the skills and inclination, but the cost and trouble can be considerable. Or you can hire somebody to do it for you, but give up some of the profits in the process.

A well-chosen rental property is relatively low risk. The primary downside is *vacancy*: going without tenants. A more obscure risk would be liability issues that could plague a landlord. But, for the majority of people so inclined, owning rental property is one of the surest ways to build wealth. The steady income is appealing. Total returns can trump what's available in the stock market. And when credit is tight and real estate values are down, rental property can still be a strong investment because it produces steady income.

In my opinion, the most important ingredient for success in rental real estate, aside from choosing properties with positive cash flow, is *knowing yourself.* Do you like *houses*: designing them, shopping for them, building them, and maintaining them? Do you like working directly with all kinds of people: on their good days, and *bad* days? Then perhaps you are cut out to be a landlord.

Though it wasn't my path to wealth, I know many others who either enhanced or built their wealth, and retirement income, by investing in rental real estate. If you like the concept, but want to remain hands off, you can always invest in a real estate or REIT mutual fund or ETF, like I do. Just understand that by taking that route, you are essentially hiring a property manager, and sharing some of the profits with them.

Take Action

- Cultivate a great relationship with your partner. Your personal finances will reflect your personal relationships.

- Slash recurring expenses mercilessly: utilities, insurance, subscriptions, memberships.

- Think long term. For every financial decision, ask yourself: "What is most economical in the long run?" Often that means saving longer, and buying quality.

- Cultivate small luxuries to feel pampered.

- Be willing to be different. Don't get attached to the appearance of your house or vehicle.

- Scrutinize your living situation, and look ahead: Do everything possible to stay in one home for an extended period. This might mean buying a little larger at first, and living more modestly later.

- Continue adding to the skill set for your profession or career, as long as you're employed.

- Make an ongoing commitment to educating yourself about all personal finance matters, and becoming a confident investor.

- Choose a mechanism to boost your income that fits your style: value investing, starting a business, or acquiring rental property.

Conclusion

"I've been rich and I've been poor. Believe me, honey, rich is better." — Sophie Tucker

How to Retire Early

I didn't set out to retire early. But I never stopped looking for more freedom in my life. Even though I had a rewarding career and was passionate about my work at times, freedom was always way more important to me than career advancement or material possessions. There was never any doubt in my mind that I would retire as soon as feasible.

Now, more than 50 years down the road, I can see the *core principles* that helped me, and can also help you, to become financially independent, and retire sooner. I found that financial independence is made up of one part *family* support, one part *career* choices, one part *money* management, and one part *personal* habits and attitudes. It's not a quick or easy process, but there are things that you can work on and improve *every* day!

If you were fortunate to be born into a family that values integrity, economy, and hard work, be grateful. If not, do your best to create that environment around you now. Build a stable, long-term relationship with a partner who shares your financial values. For me, it was only possible to make significant financial progress on the basis of a secure and joyful marriage.

Do work that you love. Identify your gifts, and find a career path that leverages those. If possible, pursue a high-paying career in a technical field. If that's not possible, at least be aware of the financial implications of your college education choices. Look for mentors and long-term professional relationships that complement your skills and personality. Be prepared to work hard, very hard, at certain points in your career. Value communication skills – written and spoken. And get along well with others.

As we've discussed, live on less than you make. Track and be aware of your expenses. Figure out the few areas where you should indulge to enjoy life. Spend there, and cut back mercilessly everywhere else. Ignore what others do. Avoid debt and pay off loans early whenever possible. Max out retirement contributions. Put raises and bonuses into investments, not a fancier lifestyle. Pursue financial education. Find a mentor, in person or in print, to help you become a confident investor. Adhere to a few bedrock investing principles: diversification, patience, simplicity, low expenses. Compute your net worth regularly.

Cultivate patience. Take life one day at a time. Financial independence is not going to be achieved quickly, even in the best of circumstances. It will require discipline, work, and persistence over a period of many years. Take care not to sacrifice quality of life in the present, for a distant future that isn't going to materialize the way you envision anyway. Never postpone quality time with your loved ones, even if it means working longer in the end. When in doubt: *Make today count, and put off retirement a little longer.*

My Story, Continued...

In this book you've learned the tools to achieve financial freedom earlier and retire as soon as possible. If you develop and maintain your financial dashboard, understand and focus on your retirement goals, learn the tools to save and invest your money, then follow my tips for cutting your expenses and boosting your income – you will retire years ahead of schedule.

What will you do with your newfound freedom?

Here's how it's working out for me: Retirement has been everything I had hoped and planned. I no longer begin each day with somebody else's agenda. I do whatever I want, without worrying about a paycheck.

The time since leaving my full-time job has been a mixture of bliss and excitement. With space and time in my life like never before, I started right away to catch up on old dreams and start new ones. Just weeks after leaving my job, we visited old friends who live on one of the less-developed islands in the Bahamas. We enjoyed hiking, snorkeling, deep-sea fishing, and boating around some of the finest oceanfront scenery in the world.

Since then we've spent many months on the road, living out of our camper van, going where we want, seeing what we want, on our own schedule. We've visited virtually all of our family and friends across the country. We've rock climbed in New Hampshire and Wyoming, mountain biked in Maine and Colorado and Arizona, and toured amazing national parks like Acadia, Dinosaur, and Mesa Verde.

But it hasn't all been recreation. I'm actually more productive now that there are no longer any obstacles to pursuing my dreams. I've ramped up my cooking skills, doing most of the grocery shopping and food preparation in our household since my retirement. I've stepped up my long-term reading interest in spirituality and psychology, and have attended several retreats. I've vastly improved my technical skills with new web technologies.

And my biggest new project is what you see right here. I've always loved to write. Now I've taken it to another level by starting the *Can I Retire Yet?* blog, and publishing my first book. I found I have a lot to offer others about saving more, investing smarter, and retiring sooner, and that people are interested in reading what I have say.

Discussing these important life issues with my readers, understanding their needs, researching and creating answers in a dynamic format that will live on and help many more people has been my most exciting professional journey in years. Most importantly, it's connected me to a network of savvy, fascinating people who are making a difference in the world.

And now it's your turn. The process of becoming financially independent can improve your life, and the lives of others, starting today, by helping you focus on what really matters. Every expense, every dollar, every hour, is measured against the question: *"Is this taking me toward or away from true freedom?"*

Once you become financially independent, all the activities, projects, and goals that were once out of reach, become possible. Your dreams will come down out of the clouds to rest in your own hands at last. Time and resources may still be finite, but you will have enough to do what you really want. As a result, you'll break out of old, stale patterns and discover new people, places, and things. As you gain new skills and experiences, you'll become more interesting to others, and more new contacts and opportunities will enter your life. Financial freedom will become a self-reinforcing cycle.

Why not start today?

Feedback

If you found this book helpful, please tell others by rating and reviewing it on Amazon. Just describe what insights were most useful, and how they helped you. And *thank you*: I value and appreciate your support very much!

If you have any concerns, or ideas for future editions, please contact me personally. My goal is to deliver great value via simple, practical, real-world wisdom. Your feedback is essential to let me know how I'm doing. I'm always interested in hearing questions and suggestions from readers. I review every message, and reply to as many as possible.

You can reach me by email at:

darrow@caniretireyet.com

Regards,

Darrow Kirkpatrick

CanIRetireYet.com

Acknowledgments

My financial education began with the rock-solid foundation bestowed by my parents, who taught me integrity, economy, and the value of work.

Most of my material success in life began when I met John Haestad. Thank you, John, for the opportunities, and the lessons, over so many years.

And thanks to my colleagues at Haestad Methods and Bentley Systems, some of the brightest and most dedicated software engineers in the world. I am deeply grateful for the role each of you played in my own journey.

I owe an enormous debt to Richard C. Young and his *Intelligence Report* which was my mentor in patient, diversified, low-cost passive index investing.

In my new role as financial blogger, I have been humbled by the generosity of the personal finance community. I am particularly indebted to Mike Piper, Todd Tresidder, Doug Nordman, Mr. Money Mustache, and Farnoosh Torabi for their early support of my efforts, and my message.

No other person played a bigger role in the creation of this book than my editor Meghan Stevenson. I have her insight and experience to thank for much of the structure, and attention to readers' needs. Any remaining shortcomings are entirely my own.

In the beginning and the end, my wife Caroline has enthusiastically supported and been part of this project as she has so many others before, and my son Alex has continued to encourage and inspire me. My journey, my successes, my life, are inseparable from theirs.

About the Author

Darrow Kirkpatrick is an author, software engineer, and investor who participated in several technology startups and retired at age 50. He is married to a schoolteacher and the father of an amazing artist and engineer. He is an experienced rock climber and enthusiastic mountain biker, and writes regularly about saving, investing, and retiring at *CanIRetireYet.com*

Index

401k 33, 51, 62, 68
4% Rule 47, 48, 93, 99

A

account 13, 16, 17, 28, 29, 31, 32, 36, 50, 52, 53, 62, 65, 66, 70,
        71, 73, 75, 77, 87, 109, 128
active management 68, 77, 80, 81, 123
annuities 33, 35, 50, 68, 71, 79
asset allocation 3, 79, 82, 83, 84, 85, 87

B

bank 15, 19, 29, 31, 32, 63, 64, 66, 67, 87, 128, 130
bonds 27, 29, 67, 70, 80, 82, 83, 84, 85, 86, 87, 123
broker 34, 73, 76
budget 14, 16, 17, 18, 20, 21, 22, 24, 25, 37, 43, 44, 49, 55, 56,
        58, 102, 104, 119, 120
Buffett, Warren 124
business 11, 29, 36, 45, 51, 62, 72, 75, 77, 81, 90, 91, 107, 108,
        109, 111, 118, 122, 123, 125, 126, 127, 128, 129, 130,
        131, 133

C

car 8, 26, 27, 54, 56, 57, 63, 64, 104, 105, 116, 124
career 8, 29, 31, 43, 47, 48, 49, 58, 81, 93, 103, 111, 122, 123,
        126, 133, 134, 135
cash 11, 13, 14, 15, 28, 31, 32, 33, 62, 64, 70, 71, 82, 83, 84, 85,
        91, 94, 102, 103, 108, 109, 123, 132
CDs 33, 66, 67
CFP 79
Charles Schwab 73
checking 17, 28, 31, 33, 65, 66, 70
cost of living 10, 11, 46, 53, 54, 57, 59
CPI 53, 55, 56

D

debt 4, 20, 26, 27, 28, 31, 32, 33, 35, 36, 37, 62, 64, 91, 100, 107, 135, 140
dining 22, 23, 102, 103
diversification 80, 125, 135

E

education 6, 26, 53, 91, 94, 122, 135, 140
emergency 64, 66, 87
ETFs 70, 80, 81, 125, 132
expense 3,4,5,7,9,10,11,12, 13,14,15,18,19,20,21,22,24, 28, 30,34,37, 43, 46, 48,49,51, 55, 52, 58, 59, 60, 63, 65, 75, 95, 97, 98, 99, 100, 101, 112, 113, 114, 116, 119, 138

F

Fidelity 73, 74, 87
financial advisor 4, 9, 75, 81, 85
financial services 1, 3, 17, 61, 72
food 22, 23, 44, 53, 55, 56, 64, 95, 101, 102, 105, 116, 117, 137
freedom 1, 2, 6, 30, 37, 41, 90, 94, 95, 104, 134, 136, 138
frugality 4, 89, 91, 116

G

generosity 120, 122, 140
Graham, Benjamin 124
groceries 13, 18, 22, 23, 44, 102

H

health 23, 57, 101, 105, 106, 109 114
health care 51,57,95,105,108
home 22, 23, 26, 34, 35, 45, 46, 51, 67, 108, 112-113 114-115 133
home equity 23, 33, 51, 67, 130
home improvements 68, 100

P

Q

R

S

27002282R00086

Made in the USA
Middletown, DE
14 December 2015